WHEN ~~THE GOING~~ GETS TOUGH
ONLY THE TOUGH
GETS GOING

WHEN THE GOING GETS TOUGH ONLY THE TOUGH GETS GOING

KAGELO HENRY RAKWENA

Outskirts Press, Inc.
Denver, Colorado

With gratitude and delight I dedicate this book to my wife, Boitumelo, B2, in celebration of our companionship. It is hard to imagine this book — or life — without her presence and love.

I also dedicate this book to the girls, Kanelo and Tetelo, to know that "When the going gets tough only the tough gets going."

Contents

Acknowledgements

Introduction

Chapter 1:
Challenges are Common Denominators 1

Chapter 2:
His Grace is Sufficient............................... 15

Chapter 3:
The Power of His Cross............................. 29

Chapter 4:
The Power of His Resurrection 47

Chapter 5:
The Just Shall Live by Faith 65

Chapter 6:
He Tested Abraham's Faith 79

Chapter 7:
Do You Also Want to Go Away?................ 99

Chapter 8:
Jehoshaphat and His Enemies 111

Chapter 9:
Challenges Are Like a Quarry 125

Chapter 10:
No More Sea... 137

Notes 151

Acknowledgements

Writing this book was not a solitary experience. Therefore, I wish to take this moment to thank the following individuals for making this book possible. First and foremost, my sincere thanks go to my wife, Boitumelo Rakwena, and the girls, Kanelo and Tetelo, for their support, prayers and allowing me to take family time to make this project possible.

Many thanks go to Mr. and Mrs. Tlhomelang and Mr. Maungo Mokotedi for reading the first draft of this book, and for their insights and prayers. To my friends and fellow believers in Botswana, for their encouragements and prayers.

My gratitude also goes to Edna Maye Loveless for editing, proofreading and for her timely insights during the process of writing this book. To Brenda Market-Green, for reviewing the manuscript.

Most importantly, I wish to thank the LORD for granting me the opportunity to write this book.

Introduction

.

"When the Going gets Tough only the tough gets going" reminds us that a life that is hidden in Christ is a life well secured for tough times. This is the life that "gets going" "when the going gets tough." It is a life of grace, faith and hope.

A life of grace. God's grace is like the shock absorbers in our vehicles that cushion the vehicles as they go up and down the bumps on the roads. Whenever the difficult times push us down, His grace lifts us up; we are never down forever. The grace of God takes us through the bumpy road of life that we may never bear pain alone, for grace cushions the pain all the way.

A life of faith. Faith is the life cord that connects us to the Source of our being. It is through faith that we receive strength and the courage to stand when storms rage and the angry winds blow about our existence. Faith keeps us connected to our Savior in the midst of our storms.

A life of hope. It is hope that keeps us focused on the race, knowing that the finish line, the end of our pilgrimage on earth, is very near. Hope is what inspires us whenever the flames of our Christian experience grow dim as we face life's vicissitudes.

Dear reader, as you go through the pages of this book, may you be inspired, knowing that "when the going gets tough" you are "the tough" that will remain standing after every storm. God's grace never leaves you alone, your faith connects you with His infinite strength, and your hope in crossing over to the other side, will see you through whatever life may bring along.

It is my hope and prayer that we may together look back and see how God has led us in our various experiences, whenever life was tough, that we may trust and praise Him more. For some, who might be going through some tough times right now, my prayer for you is in the following song by Mosie Lister. It really says it all:

"Till the Storm Passes Over"

In the dark of the midnight have I oft hid my face,
While the storm howls above me, and there's no hiding place.

Mid the crash of the thunder, Precious Lord, hear my cry,
Keep me safe till the storm passes by.

Till the storm passes over, till the thunder sounds no more,
Till the clouds roll forever from the sky;
Hold me fast, let me stand in the hollow of Thy hand,
Keep me safe till the storm passes by.

Many times Satan whispered, "There is no need to try,
For there's no end of sorrow, there's no hope by and by"
But I know Thou art with me, and tomorrow I'll rise
Where the storms never darken the skies.

When the long night has ended and the storms come no
more,
Let me stand in Thy presence on the bright peaceful shore;
In that land where the tempest, never comes, Lord, may I
Dwell with Thee when the storm passes by.

CHAPTER 1

Challenges are Common Denominators

Mark 4:35-41

35 On the same day, when evening had come, He said to them, "Let us cross over to the other side."

36 Now when they had left the multitude, they took Him along in the boat as He was. And other little boats were also with Him.

37 And a great windstorm arose, and the waves beat into the boat, so that it was already filling.

38 But He was in the stern, asleep on a pillow. And they awoke Him and said to Him, "Teacher, do You not care that we are perishing?"

39 Then He arose and rebuked the wind, and said to the sea, "Peace, be still!" And the wind ceased and there was a great calm.

40 But He said to them, "Why are you so fearful? How is it that you have no faith?"

41 And they feared exceedingly, and said to one another, "Who can this be, that even the wind and the sea obey Him!"

Mark records that after a busy day, Jesus said to

His disciples: "Let us cross over to the other side." Tired and needing rest from a day of preaching, performing miracles and answering questions from the religious leaders, Jesus entered the boat, got a pillow and laid down to rest in the stern of the ship. As the journey commenced, a storm arose while Jesus was asleep. The Sea of Galilee is well known for its sudden and furious storms. The severity of this storm is evident in the fact that the disciples, many of whom were seasoned fishermen on this very sea, were terrified. The winds were against them, the raging and high waves were slapping the sides of the boat, repeatedly swamping over it. In this fierce storm, it was too dark to see, too noisy to hear each other as lightning and thunder un-leashed their fury. Even experienced fishermen like Peter, Andrew, James and John were wondering if they were facing the end of their lives. In the midst of the storm, the disciples battled for their lives, us-ing all their experience and resources to stay alive. Busy pulling in the sails and attempting to protect the boat from capsizing and sinking, it was clear that had they suspected this monstrous storm, they would not have attempted to cross the sea.

For some time, the disciples lost sight of the One who said, "Let us cross over to the other side." He had not said, "Let us go down at the bottom of the sea." And now He was resting, leaving His life in the Father's hands. The disciples feared for their lives even though their Master was with them in the vessel. Though physically awake, they were asleep in their faith in Christ while He was present to them in their hour of need. The miracles that He performed during the day had not prepared them for this ordeal. They had not understood yet that Jesus was the "Commander of the army of the LORD" (Joshua 5:14) and that Jesus' life was not to end in the midst of the sea. In addition, Jesus' identity as a carpenter probably prevented their thinking that He could help them once the storm broke.

Jesus was physically in the vessel, but the ride was not smooth for His obedient disciples. The disciples had given up everything to follow the Son of God. They had left their careers, families and friends to follow Jesus. James and John had left a prosperous fishing industry with their father; Matthew had left his official post as a tax collector to follow Jesus. And now they were doing exactly what Jesus had instructed them to do by getting into the boat and crossing to the other side. Perhaps, this is what made it difficult for the disciples to understand why Jesus would be sleeping in the midst of a dangerous storm. Indeed, enduring life's storms when they followed the Master's will seemed greater than the storms they had faced before they met Him!

In their desperation, the disciples awakened Jesus and uttered words of bitter disappointment with Him, "Teacher, do you not care that we are perishing?" They were wondering, "What is going on? We have left everything and here we are following your instructions, and you left us alone battling for our lives. Don't you care about what we are going through now? Can't you see that we are about to drown?" They were suffering feelings of abandonment and perhaps even of resentment over their plight.

Before Jesus responded to the disciples' question, "Teacher, do you not care that we are perishing?" He first dealt with their outside problem, the storm. Jesus did not merely quiet the wind and the waves; He rebuked them. He addressed nature as if talking to a disobedient being and expecting it to hear and obey. As He raised His voice against the storm and said, "Peace, be still," there was immediate peace; the winds and waves obeyed Him. His manner of rebuking the storm, similar to his rebuke of a demon possessing a man He would meet on shore, suggests that Satan was the author of the storm. After dealing with the outside problem, Jesus responded to His disciples' question by asking them a question, "Why are you so fearful? How is it that you have no faith?" For Jesus, the storm to be feared most is the storm of unbelief, lack of faith inside, rather than the outside storm.

Jesus' question, "Why are you so fearful? How is it that you have no faith?" reveals the disciples' main problem: failure to trust in Jesus' care. Jesus challenged His disciples, "Why didn't you trust me? After all I have said and done before you, you still have no faith, even when I am with you in the vessel? I didn't forsake you during the storm, but you abandoned Me. You didn't trust my words that we would arrive on the other side."

The disciples were now entertaining a new fear, and they asked, "Who can this be, that even the wind and the sea obey Him!" Instead of searching their hearts, they continued to muse on their ignorance regarding their Master and His ways.

Interestingly, as soon as Jesus and the disciples arrived on the other side of the lake, a demon-possessed man declared, "What have I to do with You, Jesus, Son of the Most High God? I implore you by God that you do not torment me" (Mark 5:7). While the disciples were still asking one another in unbelief, "Who can this be, that even the wind and the sea obey Him?" Jesus would continue to calm the storms in their lives when they would permit Him entrance on the inside. It's important to release our fears to Jesus, aware that the rest of His creation, even the demons, bows down before His majesty and power.

The disciples' fearfulness, arising from a lack of faith in Jesus, was preventing a close connection with Him. On another occasion (Matthew 14: 31), Jesus told Peter that he had started to sink as he was walking on the water because he lacked faith.

Later (Matthew 16:8) Jesus rebuked His disciples once again for their meager faith when they worried about securing an adequate supply of bread. The disciples' fear during the storm arose because they lacked faith. They were so concerned about the storm that they lost their confidence in Jesus. Lack of faith breeds a nagging fear. Insert faith, and fear disappears as we depend on Jesus, who can see us through our difficult circumstances.

There is a familiar chorus that says:

With Jesus in the vessel, we can smile at the storm,
Smile at the storm, smile at the storm,
With Jesus in the vessel, we can smile at the storm,
As we are sailing home,
Sailing, sailing home,
Sailing, sailing home,
With Jesus in the vessel, we can smile at the storm,
As we are sailing home.

This familiar song is easy to sing, believe and enjoy when there is no storm; we should try appropriating its truth during a storm. When sailing over a calm sea, it is easy to speak of Jesus' ability to keep us in the storm; it is another thing altogether to exercise that ability when the storm is actually raging around us. It is like singing this familiar gospel song, "Jesus saves, Jesus saves" while in the church building, but walk out without salvation. It is easy to sing these truths but difficult to appropriate the messages into our experiences. And yet Jesus is ever the same, as in the case of the disciples, to look beyond the faults of His followers and see their needs, even before He would rebuke their lack of faith. In the storm and in the calm, in sickness and in health, in poverty and in abundance, in pressure and in ease, His followers have the privilege of clinging to Him by faith to draw from Him unlimited supplies for daily needs.

Returning to the disciples, we find that they did two things very well. First, instead of jumping overboard, they remained in the vessel. None of the disciples suggested jumping overboard to save their lives; if it was bad in the vessel, it was worse outside. Jumping outside would have meant leaving Jesus in the boat, and life without the master of the sea, winds and other elements would have been unbearable. Even though they may have taken some time before they awakened Jesus, who was only a carpenter, without the navigation skills of a fishermen possessed by several of them, all remained on board. We may draw a parallel here: when the journey gets tough and we question the prudence of Jesus' direction, it's important to retain our belief in His ways and wisdom. With the Lord in our vessel, we can sail through the storm.

Additionally, though the disciples grieved the Lord by their lack of faith, when they were at their wits' end, nevertheless, they turned to Him. They brought to the Lord their need, their lack of faith and their fears, not to anyone else. In spite of their weaknesses, they called on the Lord, and He quickly demonstrated that He was willing to pursue His will in their lives. Though they were not where they should have been (spiritually), they were with Jesus, the One who could heal their shortcomings. And for sure, when the Lord was done with them, later on, their fears disappeared and they even laid down their very lives for His course.

From the experience of the disciples, we understand that hard times on planet earth are part of the deal, part of life, and they are an indispensable reality to human existence. Each time hard times come, they challenge the core of our relationship with Jesus Christ. Hard times can promote spiritual growth, if we consider them to be a call to revisit our vows or commitment; in sickness and in health, in good times and bad times, rather than a call to spiritual death. Our relationship with Christ should be stronger than our circumstances, deeper than our pain, higher than our billows, closer than our enemies and more lasting than our fears. Winds, storms and waves might build a wall between us and our Lord; the darkness might hide His face from us and add fear of apparent defeat, but He is still there for us and on our side.

Further, Christianity is not an insulating tape, which would protect us from the electrical sparks that we might experience as we get in touch with life's circumstances. Rather, in Christianity we have a Companion who is willing to travel with us through life, providing comfort, guidance, and a safe haven during storms. While the ship of Zion (our faith in the Lord) might take us through some storms, the pilot of our ship, though He might appear to be asleep and uninterested in our affairs, has never failed to lead His vessels to safety. With our faith anchored in the Lord, we can be sure that our tomorrow is in His hands and our today is His yesterday, because He never lets His children travel on the way He has not been before. Since Jesus is never caught up in a storm unprepared, we have adequate reason to continue to trust Him.

We are, therefore, assured of His presence in our life vessels but not assured what might occur before we arrive at the other side. Storms may buffet us, but we are assured a safe arrival on the "other side". Our ship will not sink between the now and then. When God seems to be absent and Satan seems to be in charge of our circumstances, we can abandon trust in our human skills and fellow men, remembering the One who said, "Let us cross over to the other side." We need a reminder that unlike the disciples, we do not have to battle the storms by ourselves but should remember the One who said, "Let us go this way."

> Christianity is not an insulating tape, which would protect us from the electrical sparks that we might experience as we get in touch with life's circumstances. Rather, in Christianity we have a Companion who is willing to travel with us through life, providing comfort, guidance, and a safe haven during storms. While the ship of Zion (our faith in the Lord) might take us through some storms, the pilot of our ship, though He might appear to be asleep and uninterested in our affairs, has never failed to lead His vessels to safety.

An encounter with trouble tells us that we are not home or on the other side yet. The storm and the waves reminded the disciples that the journey was not over yet. Trouble tells us that the great controversy between God and Satan, between good and evil, is still on. And for Christians, they remind us that we are strangers and pilgrims here, waiting for a country that has no storms.

Unfortunately, Christianity or moral excellence does not make us immune from suffering, from pain and from facing life's challenges. Both believers and non-believers experience suffering of one kind or another—diseases, sickness, accidents and bereavement, the sting of poverty and hunger, political instability and wars, social discrimination and isolation and other evils that face the human race. In fact, by becoming a Christian, we enlist ourselves on God's side while becoming Satan's enemies on the other. When we decide to put on the wings of moral excellence, we'll encounter others who oppose our direction. Commitment to integrity and moral living do not elicit the applause of the crowd. The most virtuous have been misunderstood, made fun of and even sentenced to death.

As Christians, we sometimes harbor a false sense of security; a belief that when we are on the side of God, the ride will be fine. In reality, challenges may arise precisely because we are on God's side. If we do not meet the devil on our way, we may be going the same direction with him, a dire thought, because the devil never guarantees protection to his servants! Many times we forget that we have not been promised a safe ride through the ocean of life, but our Companion will not leave or forsake us during the ride. Jesus said to His disciples, "Let us cross over to the other side." If He mentions the "other side," we know it's a reality even before we get there. But before we arrive, we should not be surprised by storms, demons and winds, and yet in the apparent absence of God, the master, is still in the very ship where we are.

During stormy times Satan whispers, "You are the only one suffering, abandoned by friends and by God too! Your load is too much and life was never meant to be like this. Just give up. After all, God and people will understand your situation." But we have a message as well from God: "You are not alone; I am with you. You are not in this giant storm to perish, but to gain glorious victories which shall crown your master as the greatest and prepare you for more victories in the future. Don't give up. I am beside you and I will never leave you." During our troubles we have a choice: listen to God's or Satan's voice.

If we choose to distinguish between the storm, that assails us, and the Lord who protects, guides and remains with us through the storm, we can gain a perspective. Our attention to the Lord should evoke the moments when we made baptismal vows and the growth that Christianity affords; it presents us with opportunity to revisit false expectations and religious formulas/socializations that need to be adjusted.

One artist says he has observed that when a chicken falls, due to any emergency, it more than likely falls on its back, because its knees are at the back. Unlike chickens, human beings' knees are in front, so whenever we are to fall, we should fall forward on our knees, whenever the going gets tough. This artist puts this perspective so well in this song:

Chorus:
When the going is tough don't fall on your back,
Rather fall on your knees and things will be all right

I know you have mountains waiting for you, you cannot climb,
So you tell yourself, that you have rivers in front of you, you can
not cross,
Please don't fear, don't give up, Christ your fellow is by your side
Please don't fret, don't give up, Christ your fellow is by your side

There is no problem too big for God to solve,
Cast all your cares upon Him who cares for you,
In everything give thanks to God; just hold your peace, the
battle is His,
In everything give thanks to God; just hold your peace, the
battle is His,
When the going is tough, when the going is tough,
Never, never, never, never give up; rather fall on your knees,
No weapon formed against you shall prosper; he who rises
against you shall fall,
Fall on your knees.... [1]

CHAPTER 2

His Grace is Sufficient

2Corinthians12:7-10

7 And lest I should be exalted above measure by the abundance of the revelations, a thorn in the flesh was given to me, a messenger of Satan to buffet me, lest I be exalted above measure.

8 Concerning this thing I pleaded with the Lord three times that it might depart from me.

9 And He said to me, "My grace is sufficient for you, for My strength is made perfect in weakness." Therefore most gladly I will rather boast in my infirmities, that the power of Christ may rest upon me.

10 Therefore I take pleasure in infirmities, in reproaches, in needs, in persecutions, in distresses, for Christ's sake. For when I am weak, then I am strong.

Hard times, troubles, challenges or crisis, whatever you might choose to call them, are not a new phenomenon. Men and women of God, in both the Old and New Testament eras and during subsequent centuries, have faced life's challenges. Each had burdens of some kind, disappointments to go through. Their experiences are chronicled in the Bible to provide strength for those coming after them so that they will not lose heart by what they are called to endure.

Paul called his trials a thorn in his flesh that continually made him uncomfortable. In His darkest moments, Jesus spoke of a cup He was to drink. In no sense deserving the sufferings, rejections, beatings and crucifixion, Jesus submitted to the divine plan for redeeming the lost. It is said that "he was wounded for our transgressions, he was bruised for our iniquities: the chastisement of our peace was upon him; and by his stripes we are healed" (Isaiah 53:5).

The night before the crucifixion, the Biblical record (Matthew 26:39-44) indicates that He prayed three times, asking His Father to take away the cup of suffering, rejection and betrayal. In what must have been His most desperate moments, He asked if God could save the human race through any plan other than His death, and yet He added, "nevertheless, not as I will, but as you will" (Matthew 26:39). The more He prayed that the cup be taken from Him, the more insistently the cup was pressed upon His lips to drink. After He had prayed for the third time, the original plan of the Father and Son remained intact; the Son had to go through suffering and lay down His life as a ransom for the lost. As Paul records that plan, "That is, that God was in Christ reconciling the world to Himself, not imputing their trespasses to them; and has committed to us the word of reconciliation" (2Corinthians 5:19). Both the Father and the Son were involved with the plan of redemption. The Son was not left alone to face the challenges of the crucifixion.

The record clarifies that Jesus was not alone during His betrayal, disappointments, and pain during His earthly ministry. The Father was with His Son. This provides assurance to us that no child of God goes through suffering alone. God is always by our side, though at times our tears and sorrows may block our view from His abiding presence. When at times our sorrows become like a huge mountain before us and the darkness of our circumstances may blind our view, as God was with His Son, so He will be with us no matter how steep our path might be, His sufficient grace will see us through.

In 2Corinthians12, Paul talks about his personal experience in regard to his "thorn in the flesh." Whatever the thorn was, it was something that made him extremely uncomfortable. Like his master (Jesus), Paul prayed three times for the removal of the thorn from his flesh, and three times God said "No" to Paul just as He did to His Son when He prayed in Gethsemane (Matthew 26:36-46).

Instead, God promised to supply Paul with additional grace, "My grace is sufficient." Through the experiences of Jesus and Paul we see that God's grace is stronger than our problems, circumstances, and challenges and that He will supply His sufficiency, and still let His servants drink "the bitter cup" or remain with "the thorn" in their experiences. We can conclude that sometimes God answers our prayers by supplying us with more of His strength to endure than by removing our circumstances to make us feel better.

Interestingly, Christianity is full of paradoxes. For instance, Paul declares that "when I am weak, then I am strong," meaning that in his weakness he became strong as he realized that God was the source of his strength. God becomes like a walking stick, to be our rod that we lean on to maintain our stability. We become full whenever we are empty. When we let go of our self-centeredness, God will fill us with His presence to do His will. We keep our life by losing it. That is, in Christ, we consider ourselves dead (dead to sin and to the worldly pleasures) while at the same time our life is hid in His life, so that at the end we may have life in abundance. Through the experience of Paul, God demonstrates that we can become strong in our weakness by realizing that in our insufficiency God is our strength, meeting all our needs and calming all our fears.

Although the ministry of Christ illustrates God's concern for suffering and His power to relieve it, heaven's essential concern lies in empowering change in us, not in our circumstances. God specializes in changing and equipping us so that we are able to face our challenges rather than changing our circumstances to suit us. His grace has a way of pulling us from "under circumstances" and placing us "on top of circumstances." After all, does not the Bible say He "prepares a table [a banquet, or a feast] before me in the presence of my enemies?" (Psalms 23:5). In our words, "He gives me success while my enemies are watching; my enemies become the audience as God blesses me." Our enemies, therefore, upon hearing of our successes, would be conquered by their hatred, envy and jealousy — from their inside to their outside — long before even God and circumstances would reach them.

We can conclude that God specializes in changing, or equipping, us to live above our circumstances, rather than changing our circumstances to suit us; He specializes in making us, His servants, stronger than our enemies, rather than in making our enemies weaker than us. God's grace, therefore, could multiply our resources, strengthening our abilities without decreasing our enemies' resources and weapons. Our concern is neither how strong our enemies are, nor how difficult our circumstances are, but who is on our side. For with God, we will be more than able to cope.

Perhaps that is why the Bible says that "But those who wait upon the LORD shall renew their strength; they shall mount up with wings as eagles; they shall run, and not be weary; and they shall walk, and not faint" (Isaiah 40:31). Those who do not hope (wait or trust) in the Lord have no further supply of strength or resources to renew their strength. Their envy, jealousy and hatred become a burden, a stumbling block for their own success. Sometimes success and prosperity lie not in the change of our circumstances, overcoming our enemies, or dealing with the storm, but in the fact that God, through His grace provides strength to fly above the storm like an eagle at a level where the storm no longer has effect on our being. His grace places us where the missiles from our enemies cannot reach us; our enemies become the audience, or spectators, of our success.

Making a very practical application, isn't it likely that God will work to change us to suit our spouses, rather than changing our spouses to suit us? We might be tempted to work hard to change others to be compatible with our desires, but we will find that the most accessible object for change is our-selves. Indeed, conventional wisdom says the only person you can change is yourself. Therefore, an apt prayer could be, "Lord, change me," or "Lord, equip me," or "Lord, make me, prepare me, to be the best life partner that you can create in me." It is interesting that we would pray for and wish other people's sons and daughters to change while we ourselves are not subject to needed changes. I would think that if God could answer such prayers we would do well to answer our own prayers first!

By the way, this is not a treatise on marital relationships or how to find a life partner, but about our perceptions in regard to our troubles and how God sometimes intervenes in human affairs. However, using marital relationships as an example, we find that Christians sometimes venture into forbidden grounds, making decisions that are not sanctioned by God, and that sooner or later result in scars, disease, pain and suffering that could have been prevented or avoided. There remain shame, guilt, and self-condemnation, lack of self-forgiveness, remorse and feelings of emptiness without God's presence and peace. Even for such ones, God's grace is still sufficient; the fountain of His love, and of His Son's blood, has not lost its power.

Even if God does not remove the scars of where we have been, of what we have eaten and drunk, or violate the freedom of our unbelieving spouses whom we had married regardless of His counsel, He would still want to change us from inside out to enable us to face our situations. Our scars could tell others, especially the young: "Don't go there, don't eat and drink that." Our staying with God could tell those who are observing: "His grace is sufficient. You too can be accepted." No matter where we have been, or where the devil has taken us, we are not of the devil; he did not create anyone of us and he has no eraser (blood) to deal with our past.

We can conclude that God specializes in changing, or equipping, us to live above our circumstances, rather than changing our circumstances to suit us; He specializes in making us, His servants, stronger than our enemies, rather than in making our enemies weaker than us. God's grace, therefore, could multiply our resources, strengthening our abilities without decreasing our enemies' resources and weapons. Our concern is neither how strong our enemies are, nor how difficult our circumstances are, but who is on our side. For with God, we will be more than able to cope.

Only God has the eraser, the blood of His Son, to deal with our past and enabling us to live above our past and present circumstances. His grace, God's wonderful and amazing grace, is sufficient.

If we find ourselves fighting furiously with our circumstances and inviting God to do the same, we may fail to recognize that God's purpose is to mold us into His similitude for His sovereign purposes. As we pray that God will take care of our problems, do we consider that we might be the greatest problem, hindrance, that He has to take care of first before He deals with whatever we are asking Him to attend to? Can we pray, "I am waiting to be broken and remolded so that whenever my situation is taken care of, I will be strong enough to handle the blessings, and my heart will be ready to give you all the praise?" The alternative is to find God busy changing our circumstances and other people while we remain unchanged, weak, and with the same perceptions, refusing to take responsibility for our actions.

Therefore, it's time to let the thorns and thistles grow up on our way while letting God give us the shoes to walk tall on the same path. We let the thunderstorm roar and the lightning flash, but let Him give us wings to fly above the storm. We allow our enemies to encompass us, but let God prepare a banquet for us in the midst of our enemies. After all, we live by His grace, not by our best efforts or our weapons; we live by His grace, not by our wisdom or good reasoning. We live by His merits, and not even by our own righteousness. We do not even live by our promises to Him, but by His promises to us. If He does not remove the problems that we face, therefore, it is a matter of endurance, and we need courage and His grace (His abiding presence) to go on in spite of whatever is in our way.

We have Paul's testimony that as he grew in grace, he learned that negative circumstances could be a call to trust his Creator. Likewise, negative circumstances could be a call to us to depend more fully upon God's resources rather than on our efforts, a call to know Him better, and a call to the awareness that He is still in charge. Whenever things go wrong, they could be a reminder that even at our very best in a relationship with God, the devil will still knock at the door of our spiritual dwelling. We never arrive where the devil can not knock at the door to tempt us. In Gethsemane, imagine the devil's knocking at temptation's door to say to Jesus, "Why should you have to suffer? You don't need to go through all these." For Paul, the devil must have laughed at him, "If you are His instrument, why can't He remove the thorn from your flesh?" God answers these challenges: "I specialize not in changing circumstances to suit you, but rather, in increasing your capacity, resources and stamina to endure and to suit circumstances. My grace is sufficient, for my power is manifested more whenever there is an apparent defeat."

For years, Christians have found solace and strength from hymns of experience. In addition to characters in the Bible, we are thankful to song writers who have testified through their songs how to find strength in weakness. Their songs form summaries of their individual experiences as they found God's grace in the midst of their pain and suffering, and acceptance in God from their waywardness and from their problems. One such artist, Charlotte Elliot, lived between 1789 and 1861 in England. Though Charlotte lived to be eighty-two years old, most of her adult life was lived in great physical suffering. Before the age of thirty, she had pursued a carefree life, without God, and had become a popular artist. As she became physically sick, she became depressed, without peace of mind.

Charlotte accepted the Lord as her Savior in 1822, during the visit of a Swiss evangelist, Dr. Caesar Malan, in England. Malan challenged Charlotte, "You must come just as you are, a sinner, to the Lamb of God, who takes away the sin of the world." Though sick and bedridden, she achieved peace of mind, knowing that the One who accepted her stood by her bedside day after day. She could, therefore, testify, "He knows, and He alone, what it is day after day, hour after hour, to fight against bodily feelings of almost overpowering weakness, languor and exhaustion, to resolve not to yield to slothfulness, depression and instability, such as the body causes me to indulge, but to rise every morning determined to take for my motto, 'If a man will come after Me, let him deny himself, take up his cross daily, and follow Me.'" And at another time she added, "God sees, God guides, God guards me. His grace surrounds me, and His voice continually bids me to be happy and holy in His service just where I am." She put her experience of dealing with pain and finding comfort in knowing that God is with us in our pains, into the hymn, "Just As I Am."

Just as I am, without one plea, But that Thy blood was shed for me,
And that Thou bidst me come to Thee, O Lamb of God, I come, I come.

Just as I am, and waiting not to rid my soul of one dark blot,
To Thee whose blood can cleanse each spot, O Lamb of God, I come, I come.

Just as I am, though tossed about with many a conflict, many a doubt,
Fightings and fears within, without, O Lamb of God, I come, I come.

Just as I am, poor, wretched, blind; Sight, riches, healing of the mind,
Yea, all I need in Thee to find, O Lamb of God, I come, I come.

Just as I am, Thou wilt receive, Wilt welcome, pardon,
   cleanse, relieve;
Because Thy promise I believe, O Lamb of God, I come,
   I come.

Just as I am, Thy love unknown hath broken every barrier
   down;
Now, to be Thine, yea, Thine alone, O Lamb of God, I
   come, I come.[1]

CHAPTER 3

The Power of His Cross

**Matthew chapters 26 and 27;
Mark chapters 14 and 15**

**Luke chapters 22 and 23;
John chapters 18 and 19**

Matthew 27:35-42

35 Then they crucified Him, and divided His garments, casting lots, that it might be fulfilled which was spoken by the prophet: *"They divided My garments among them, And for My clothing they cast lots."*

36 Sitting down, they kept watch over Him there.

37 And they put up over His head the accusation written against Him: THIS IS JESUS THE KING OF THE JEWS.

38 Then two robbers were crucified with Him, one on the right and another on the left.

39 And those who passed by blasphemed Him, wagging their heads

40 and saying, "You who destroy the temple and build *it*

in three days, save Yourself! If You are the Son of God, come down from the cross."

41 Likewise the chief priests also, mocking with the scribes and elders, said,

42 "He saved others; Himself He cannot save. If He is the King of Israel, let Him now come down from the cross, and we will believe Him.

All the four gospel writers recount the events of that painful and fearful Friday when Jesus suffered and died. None of the disciples were ready for this particular Friday. Jesus had tried several times to prepare them for this day, but they could not even comprehend the extent of the enmity of the religious leaders against their master and teacher. Like many other followers of Christ, the disciples thought that the kingdom of God, the Messiah's reign, the Davidic Kingdom, would come after dealing with the oppressive Romans through an earthly army, rather than dealing with sin and its oppressive power through Christ's sufferings and death on the cross. Moreover, throughout those awful hours of His suffering, the believers expected Jesus to perform a miracle at one point during the day and free Himself, proving Himself to be the Holy One and taking over the earthly political powers.

Let us remember that on Tuesday of the same week, when Jesus rode that donkey into Jerusalem, the disciples and many of His followers shouted "Hosanna to the Son of David! Blessed is He who comes in the name of the LORD! Hosanna in the highest!" (Matthew 21:9). They thought that Jesus was about to become the king, and perhaps they were excited about the prospective positions they would have in His earthly kingdom. And maybe they thought that in His kingdom the sick would be healed, food would be in abundance, and that they would be free at last from the Romans. On that Tuesday, the disciples walked tall, chests out; they felt highly honored to be associated with such a king, and they wanted the entire world to know whom they were following.

However, on Friday, their hopes were shattered. They fled for their lives, for they could not stand the shame of belonging to a master who had done so many miracles, preached with such authority, attracted so many witnesses, and yet let Himself become a victim of circumstances. Hence, they did not then want people to associate them with Jesus. It was easy to have friends on a Tuesday, when everything was fine, but not on a Friday, when the ugly, the bad, their cousins and supposed friends seemed to have come together for a show.

Before rushing to blame the disciples for their lack of preparation for that particular Friday, we need to remind ourselves that there were others who were not ready either. For instance, Judas was ready to wholesale Jesus for thirty pieces of silver, but not ready to spend his profits. The religious leaders were ready to buy Jesus, but not ready for a recall to release Him, or even to exchange Him for Barabbas. Satan was ready for the events of Friday, but unprepared for the Sunday morning. The enemies of Christ were convinced to put Him on the cross, but they failed to convince death and the grave to hold Him forever.

Sometimes our valleys, like Friday, our days of disappointments and pain, seem never to end. We forget that at the end of every valley, the ground rises again. Valleys do not last forever. Fridays come and go, though at times they leave us with scars and memories of their pain. The events of a Friday may bring us into a valley of cares and worry, robbing us of peace and happiness, but not for long. Similarly, in winter, with its chilling winds or snow, we lose perspective, forgetting that spring time will return with its warmth. We need to recall that for our Lord, Sunday will come and the events of Friday and their sting will flee away.

It was on Friday that the Savior was taken from one court to another, from shame to shame, and from mockery to mockery. He was taken before Annas, then Caiphas, then to Pilate, on to Herod and back to Pilate. He was taken from one form of abuse to another and from pain to more pain.[1] Religion and politics came together, the sacred and the secular kissed each other, with the children of light and of darkness eating from one table. Justice lingered outside the judgment hall while mercy, in the absence of a mediator, aborted inside the courthouse.

Further, in the courthouse, in the absence of true witnesses, the false witnesses multiplied and prevailed against the innocent Son of God. Jesus was twice scourged on His back for crimes He had not committed. Jesus watched as Barabbas, a criminal, was set free, and He was condemned to die instead.

Led out of the judgment hall to be crucified on mount Calvary, Jesus bore on His bleeding shoulders the cross that was prepared for Barabbas. A jeering crowd placed a thorny crown on the head of the Savior of the world. Then they hailed at Him, mocked Him as a useless king, whose followers could not defend His throne. What an awful sight!

Jesus had had no night's rest, no breakfast, no lunch, and no water to drink. He was tired, hungry, thirsty, and beaten up, but was not giving up. As He staggered toward Calvary, the weight of the cross was more than He could bear. When He fainted, the Roman soldiers looked around to see if there was any disciple, or anyone who seemed to sympathize with Jesus, to help carry the cross. No one seemed to be willing to carry the cross. At that moment, a stranger, Simon from Cyrene, met the crowd, showed some interest in the suffering man, and though he was not a disciple of Jesus, the cross was laid upon him. Side by side, Simon and Jesus ascended the mountain.

Arriving at the top of the mountain, Jesus, the Lamb of God, dedicated to take away our sins, was laid on the cross, and the rusty nails went through His flesh. Once nailed to the cross, the cross and its victim were lifted up and mercilessly plunged into a prepared hole. As for the tormentors, they continued to mock at Him, "He saved others, let Him save Himself, and we will believe in Him." Above His head they put a signboard with the words, "This is Jesus, The King of the Jews." John records that this charge was written in three languages; in Hebrew, Latin and Greek, so that many people could read it and know that the once self-proclaimed king of the Jews ended up on the cruel cross.

Jesus' death was not only a cause for celebration among the priests and teachers of the law, the soldiers and some members of the crowd, but also among those who were passing by; Satan and his demons were surely celebrating it as their victory as well. For the priests and the teachers of the law, Jesus was gone, the end of a man who caused confusion, who arrested the attention of many of their followers, and taught in a different manner. The priests were happy to remain as the main interpreters of the law and to maintain the status quo without having to compete with Jesus, who eloquently challenged their power structure.

Gambling for His clothes, the soldiers could now retire from being part of a team torturing a man whose crimes they did not understand. They had followed orders from Pilate to torture and crucify this innocent victim. They had followed evil orders before, although never to this magnitude! In fact, the Scripture records that the Roman centurion and his junior soldiers were at one point terrified by the events at the cross, and they confessed, "Truly this was the Son of God" (Matthew 27:54)! It was, therefore, a relief to those soldiers once they heard that Jesus was dead. For the soldiers, it was over; they could return to their homes.

Not all in the crowd wanted to see Jesus crucified. Some expected that Jesus would perform a miracle some time during the day and save Himself. Others, like the women from Galilee, the mother of Jesus, John, one of the disciples, and Joseph of Arimathea, showed their concern, but were powerless to rescue Jesus from His terrible ordeal (Matthew27: 55-61). Their hearts were broken; they were overwhelmed with sorrow and grief from the events of the day.

Taunters passing by the cross, like the priests, shook their heads in mockery, and shouted abuse at Jesus, "You can destroy and build the temple in three days…. Well then, save yourself and come down from the cross!" In essence they were saying, "Prove your case that you are the Messiah. Put your theory into practice and let us see it!" Both the

> God's purposes are never delayed, hurried, stopped or jeopardized by the plots of our enemies. Though He may permit some negative events in our lives, He is still in control; His purposes for our lives will still come to pass, and He will prevail in bringing us up over whatever the enemy uses to bring us down. His word is true, "And we know that all things work together for good to those who love God, to those who are the called according to His purpose" (Romans 8:28). God will, therefore, use the negatives and positives, the good and the bad that might come on our way, as platforms on which to display His glory.

priests and the jeering crowd assumed they had the upper hand with the will of God at their disposal, showing that Jesus was ignorant, and that He was far from being the Son of God, or being the Messiah He claimed to be. How strange it is that whenever things go wrong, no one asks where the devil is!

Does this sound familiar? When the going is tough, we are likely to encounter those who question our faith! They would say, "If you are a Christian, then.... And if you are a Christian, you should be.... And if there is a God in heaven, then

He should...." It is unsettling to find that those who do not know God want to give us instructions on what to do and expect when the going is tough! It is even more unsettling when we become victims of these expectations, as if we do not know God personally.

Let us put this in our minds: God is a heavyweight fighter; He would not fight in the streets to prove His skills. God is not an amateur in facing with serious threats. He is a longsuffering fighter who can endure in the ring till the last moments of the fight, because He always wins His conflicts before the conflicts begin. God knows the end from the beginning. The enemies were deceived by His bleeding, even by His death. They thought that He was knocked out. The enemies of the cross failed to realize that Jesus was just beginning to pick up His speed; this was His first day out of the three days of the fight, and on the third day they would be the ones knocked out.

Satan and his demons were another group that felt victorious, thinking they had a reason to celebrate on that Friday. They had long tried and failed to get rid of Jesus, beginning when Jesus was born. Many children were killed in an effort to kill Jesus. Subsequently, Jesus with His disciples survived many storms by sea. The devil wanted to kill Jesus before He rescued people from his oppression. But now, the devil and his demons had captured their most wanted enemy. Jesus was apparently in their hands, and all their fears were subsiding. With Jesus in their hands, there was no one to cast out demons, to heal the sick, and to turn people's hearts to the God they had long hated.

With confidence, Satan and his angels watched as the priests and soldiers secured the tomb of Jesus. A big stone was rolled in front of the entrance of the tomb, and the tomb was sealed, so that no one would steal the body of Jesus. Pilate released soldiers to guard the tomb, to avoid claims that an empty tomb meant Jesus had risen. The priests wanted to do away with all of Jesus' promises about His resurrection. They wanted to be in control and avoid any surprises.

When the tomb was secured, Satan, the master of all demons, could make his speech: "You, Son of God; I failed to defeat you in Heaven, when I was still called the Morning Star (Isaiah 14:12-14) and you were called Michael (Daniel 10:13, 21; 12:1), and I failed to destroy you when you were born, but now you are mine. You, Death, keep Him in your bosom. You, worms, consume His body for dinner, and invite others and celebrate. You, Grave, keep Him, hold Him; do not let go of Him." Thus the great deceiver powerfully deceived himself!

We may say, "That Friday was terrible. How could they do such a thing, just kill the Son of

God with no evidence of wrongdoing? That was not fair!" Of course that was not fair; one of life's bitterest lessons teaches us that in a world of sin, fairness is rare. There is no such thing as fairness when the going is tough, when we are on a Friday experience, when the Tuesday experience is long forgotten and the Sunday of our resurrection seems to be a doomed promise. Life's circumstances, or evil people, could take our only treasure, our only means of survival, and leave us without resources to meet our daily needs. We see parents who have the skills and the know-how to put bread on the table, dying before their children are prepared to meet life in the outside world. At other times, life robs a parent of a son or daughter, perhaps just graduating from college, whose promise would have rescued the family from the sting of poverty. If the devil, or life's circumstances, whatever they may be, could not cause us pain by introducing drugs, divorce, sickness and violence into our families and communities, the evil one doesn't hesitate to touch our jobs, our lands, our houses and our accounts. Friday comes upon us unprepared, at a time we would least expect. Of course it's not fair!

However, many times when the devil thinks he has a child of God, his perspective fails him. On crucifixion Friday, Satan celebrated a false success. In the first place, he had not considered that taking Jesus to the cross to stop His dreams was only putting Him in a visible position. When visiting Greeks came to Jerusalem seeking Him, Jesus had said, "And I, if I am lifted up from the earth, will draw all peoples to Myself" (John 12:32). He knew that the cross would be His platform from which all nations would be saved. Satan and the enemies of Jesus, in their mission to destroy Him, took Him and placed Him in the best saving position possible. They lifted Him high in shame and ridicule, and in the process, all eyes turned to the victim of the cross as the Savior of the entire human race. The works of Jesus' enemies put God's love for sinners in a spotlight, and the cross as the emblem of His grace toward the fallen humanity. The shameful cross was turned into being the altar of sacrifice and victory and a symbol of commitment and loyalty to the God who gave all.

Second, the inscription that was fastened above Jesus' head, "The King of the Jews," was written in Hebrew, Latin and Greek so that all could read and laugh at the victim (John 19: 19-20). The enemies of Jesus did not realize that by writing the charge against Jesus in (1) Hebrew, the language of religion, all religions would later on have evidence that Jesus is the only Rabbi who shed His innocent blood for His followers. Religion without Jesus is religion without blood that can wash away the stain of sin, shame and guilt; in (2) Latin, the language of power, a message to challenge all kings and lords to recognize the status of Jesus as the King of kings and Lord of lords; people who lead without Jesus being their Leader would take their followers to dead-ends; in (3) Greek, the language of the scholars, alerting teachers and students to the knowledge that Jesus is the incarnate Truth and the Source of all knowledge and wisdom. Jesus is the alpha and the omega, He forms the entire Greek alphabet, and He spells out the entire meaning of what life is all about. Without Jesus, teachers and students would lose the entire purpose of their learning, and their education, instead of drawing them closer to the Source, would lead them away from Him.

Third, at the cross Jesus dealt with sin and its consequences. When Jesus cried out, "My God, my God, why have you forsaken me?" (Mark 15:34), He felt the weight of the sin of the whole world, and the wrath of God against sin. Forsaken on our behalf, going through the punishment of sin on our behalf, He set us free. Jesus paid the ransom price, walked through the narrow path to open a way for us all, and showed us that sin and its works could take the Son of God to the cross. Each time we feel pressure on our shoulders, we can look at Calvary; He went there alone that we may not have to be alone whenever we bear our crosses to follow Him. Whenever we are tempted to give up, we are called to look up, for He is not only able to save, but to keep us from falling away. And whenever the going gets tough, and we get tired of the way, feeling forsaken and lonely, we can remember that He was forsaken to provide assurance that we would never be forsaken.

Lastly, the devil and the other enemies of Jesus were not helping God to save humanity. Taking Jesus to the cross did not qualify them for partnership with God. Even Jesus' enemies were killing Him as a criminal, not as one who did the will of God. God was the only one who turned the events upside down for His purposes.

It is like the enemies of Joseph, his brothers, who sold him into slavery to stop his dreams to come to pass. They sold him to be a slave but became a ruler instead. They sold Joseph, sent him to a far country, trying to avoid bowing down before their young brother as their king in the future. To their surprise, they followed Joseph and bowed down before him in that far country.

Likewise, Jesus was crucified as a criminal, but His death bridged the gap between criminals, and all other sinners, and God. The horrible display to humiliate the Son of God on Friday only made the day even more memorable and more glorious for those seeking salvation. The works of Jesus' enemies put God's love for sinners in a spotlight, and the cross as the emblem of His grace towards the fallen humanity. The shameful cross was turned into being the alter of sacrifice and victory and a symbol of commitment and loyalty to the God who gave all. Many put crosses on their dresses, necklaces, churches, offices and homes, not just to decorate but in remembrance of His saving blood.

God's purposes are never delayed, hurried, stopped or jeopardized by the plots of our enemies. Though He may permit some negative events in our lives, He is still in control; His purposes for our lives will still come to pass, and He will prevail in bringing us up over whatever the enemy uses to bring us down. His word is true, "And we know that all things work together for good to those who love God, to those who are the called according to His purpose" (Romans 8:28). God will, therefore, use the negatives and positives, the good and the bad that might come our way, as platforms on which to display His glory.

One artist puts the experience of human suffering and God's presence in the following song: "No One Ever Cared for Me Like Jesus." The artist, Charles Frederick Weigle, was both an inspiring preacher and a gifted songwriter. Charles spent most of his life as an itinerant evangelist and gospel songwriter. One day, returning home from an evangelistic crusade, he found a note left by his wife of many years. The wife simply said she had had enough of an evangelist's life and was leaving him. Charles became so despondent during the next several years that there were times when he contemplated suicide. This was his Friday experience, and his suffering was long and deep. There were moments when Charles even wondered if anyone really cared for him. After some time, his faith was again restored and he became active for the Lord again. Soon he felt compelled to write a song that would be a summary of his past tragic experience and how God cared for Him in the midst of pain. On his Friday experience, he did not carry his cross alone. Jesus, who had gone this way before, was with him.

I would love to tell you what I think of Jesus
Since I found in Him a friend so strong and true;
I would tell you how He changed my life completely,
He did something that no other friend could do.

CHORUS
No one ever cared for me like Jesus;
There's no other friend so kind as He;
No one else could take the sin and darkness from me.
O how much He cared for me!

All my life was full of sin when Jesus found me;
All my heart was full of misery and woe;
Jesus placed His strong and loving arms around me,
And He led me in the way I ought to go.

Every day He comes to me with new assurance,
More and more I understand His words of love;
But I'll never know just why He came to save me,
Till some day I see His blessed face above.[2]

CHAPTER 4

The Power of His Resurrection

Matthew 28: 1-15; Luke 24: 1-12;
John 20: 1-18;

Mark 16:1-8

1 Now when the Sabbath was past, Mary Magdalene, Mary the mother of James, and Salome bought spices, that they might come and anoint Him.

2 Very early in the morning, on the first day of the week, they came to the tomb when the sun had risen.

3 And they said among themselves, "Who will roll away the stone from the door of the tomb for us?"

4 But when they looked up, they saw that the stone had been rolled away—for it was very large.

5 And entering the tomb, they saw a young man clothed in a long white robe sitting on the right side; and they were alarmed.

6 But he said to them, "Do not be alarmed. You seek Jesus of Nazareth, who was crucified. He is risen! He is not here. See the place where they laid Him.

7 But go, tell His disciples—and Peter—that He is going

before you into Galilee; there you will see Him, as He said to you."
8 So they went out quickly and fled from the tomb, for they trembled and were amazed. And they said nothing to anyone, for they were afraid.

The Friday of the crucifixion had come and gone, but the events of the fearful day still lingered in the minds of the disciples, soldiers, chief priests, Satan and his demons. On the following day, the Sabbath, the soldiers, Satan and his mighty demons continued with their mission of watching Jesus' tomb; the chief priests went on with their ceremonies at the synagogues. Some of Jesus' disciples locked themselves in the upper room to contain their shame and fears while those who went to worship found it to be meaningless without Jesus. All parties involved were left with unanswered questions, wondering why and if they had seen the real end of Jesus, the master and teacher. There was some kind of unrest, without knowing what to expect.

That was a weekend of another kind. Never before had the universe witnessed anything like that! Even among the holy angels in heaven, one would believe that silence reigned, for their master, their creator, was lying in the tomb. The angels who sang "Hosanna in the highest" when Jesus was born remained silent during that dreadful week-end. Each holy angel waited in expectation. Would they be called by the Father to be present on planet Earth when God's Son arose from death?

In this chapter, we will look at what the four gospel writers have to say about the Sunday morning of the resurrection of our Lord Jesus Christ. We will examine the experiences of the women who went early to the tomb, of the disciples who remained behind locked doors, of the angel who came down from heaven, of the soldiers and the chief priests, and of Satan and his demons. Then we will explore some of the benefits, or the power, of the resurrection.

The women and other disciples

All four gospel writers record the visit of the women who woke up early Sunday morning, while it was still dark, to go to Jesus' tomb. They were planning to anoint His body with the perfumes that were bought on Friday, in preparation for His permanent burial. None of the women anticipated a resurrection or an empty tomb. Foremost in their minds was the prospect of performing a loving act of reverence for Jesus' body, notwithstanding its expected state of decay.

Obstacles of the darkness, the soldiers, and the big stone, and of Pilate's seal were not a discouragement to the women, though they recognized them as realities that could not be ignored. Without a plan, resources or a way of dealing with the obstacles, the women asked each other, "Who will roll away the stone from the door of the tomb for us?" (Mark 16:3). This was not a question from scared disciples who were sitting around and wondering if they could stay out of trouble, but from disciples who were on their way to face the challenges of the day no matter what they might be. They were ready to risk their lives, rise up early and start the journey in spite of the bad circumstances. Their passion to anoint Jesus' body was so strong that they did not have time to ruminate about their circumstances. We need to underline the fact that other disciples avoided the tomb, not because they believed Jesus had risen from death, but rather, because of fear, disappointment, and shame.

While we could agree that the women and the rest of the disciples did not expect Jesus to rise from the tomb, fear and shame immobilized the other disciples, whereas love for Christ propelled the women to go out. Thus, the women were among the first witnesses of the resurrection. They spoke with the angels and saw firsthand what others did not see. Their waking up was not in vain. Their faith, fears, and even their unbelief, were answered when they ventured out. All their obstacles, their circumstances, were dealt with by God when they acted; their action was a manifestation of their fearless willingness to be identified with Jesus, in contrast to those who remained in the locked room.

There are at least three insights that arise from examining the experience of the women as compared with that of other disciples. First, we have the assurance that God deals with circumstances when we stand on our faith rather than sitting on our fears. Fear that is not conquered will cripple or paralyze us, and keep us locked in our upper room of unbelief; faith, on the other hand, can give us courage to face obstacles. Unconquered, our fear will act against us as we continue to contain it. Like the presence of HIV/AIDS in the body, fear can kill our spiritual immunity system, making us vulnerable to once conquered sins and weaknesses such as selfishness, self-preservation, backsliding, unbelief and lapsing in witnessing.

Second, from the experience of the women, we can learn that whenever we walk by faith, God goes ahead of us, dealing with the obstacles, so that when we get there, our problems are taken care of. Our tomorrow, therefore, would become God's yesterday, because He would take care of our Tuesday while we would be still on our Monday. This means that we won't need not take the cares, obstacles and worries of our Tuesday and bring them over to our Monday before Tuesday comes. Further, we can rest well on His promises, going to sleep on our Monday, knowing that the God who neither slumbers nor sleeps will take care of our Tuesday; God will be there when we get there. His leading does not take us where His grace can not meet our needs. Hence, though the women woke up so early in the morning, the angel of the Lord arrived earlier than they did; they did not even see God take care of their obstacles. Because God always arrives before we do, if there be any challenges remaining, such as the Red Sea before the Israelites, we can rest assured that He has already provided a path that we can walk.

Third, faith, as a spiritual gift, does not recognize gender roles, and, as a spiritual muscle, it grows as it is exercised. While the men of the movement (Christ's movement), the leaders to be, feared for their lives, the women were out risking their lives in order to anoint the body of Jesus. Faith does not align with social structure, social identity, gender stereotypes and position; whoever exercises his/her spiritual muscle experiences muscle growth, and the ability to lift even heavier obstacles. God will roll stones away in response to an active faith. This, therefore, leaves no one out—the laity and ministers, men and women, and young and old— all can exercise their God-given faith based upon His word.

The Angel of the Lord

The Bible states that the angel of the Lord came from heaven early Sunday morning, arriving at the tomb before the women came. According to one author, the angel came from heaven at a speed faster than lightning. As Satan and his angels heard the sound of the coming angel and beheld his unspeakable glory, they fled, thinking that their day of judgment had come.[1]

Moreover, the Bible records that the appearance of the angel of the Lord "was like lightning, and his clothing as white as snow" as he landed on the ground. As a result, the guards "became like dead men" (Matthew 28:1-4). The angel of the Lord rolled away the stone from the mouth of the tomb, and welcomed the Son of God back to life.

It is important to note that the angel of the Lord did not first consult with the chief priests, Pilate or the soldiers before removing the stone, for he was sent by the monarch of the universe. Whenever the time comes for God to act on behalf of His sons and daughters, He does not consult with their enemies, and neither a devil nor the flesh would stand before His presence. God is not consulting with our bosses, superiors, teachers, and even parents, who do not believe in either our potential or resurrection (our rising up from circumstances), before He lifts us up and places us where He would like us to be.

God is never scared by those who scare us, He is never subservient to the wishes of our enemies, He is never locked into a corner which He has not seen before; in every situation He has many ways out. It is God who takes care of stones, enemies and the demons. And whenever a Sunday comes, the works of a Friday give way to the angel of the Lord.

Faith, as a spiritual gift, does not recognize gender roles, and as a spiritual muscle, it grows as it is exercised. While the men of the movement (Christ's movement), the leaders to be, feared for their lives, the women were out risking their lives in order to anoint the body of Jesus. Faith does not align with social structure, social identity, gender stereotypes and position; whoever exercises his/her spiritual muscle experiences muscle growth and ability to lift even heavier obstacles. God will roll stones away in response to an active faith.

Further, the resurrection of our Lord Jesus Christ was a surprise to His friends and enemies alike. They had heard what He said about His death and resurrection, but it came as a surprise when it happened. It was an unexpected event, amazing and more glorious than mortals could ever imagine. The resurrection could not be faked or ignored, as if it had not happened. And it was crystal clear to both friends and enemies that the body of Jesus had not been stolen by anybody. This gives us assurance that whenever God blesses, He employs unique ways, clarifying that the Almighty is at work. Counterfeits of the works of God may come in some instances, but their worth will be tested and revealed by the passing of time.

The Soldiers and the Chief Priests

As the angel of the Lord arrived at the tomb, the mission of the soldiers guarding the body of Jesus was over. The angel had come to do the impossible; to face Satan and his demons, to take care of the soldiers and Pilate's seal, to roll away the stone and welcome the living Jesus. Though the soldiers remained "like dead men," they witnessed and heard everything during the resurrection.

After the soldiers saw the powerful events of the resurrection as firsthand witnesses, they exchanged their true testimony for money. While the women were on their way to the tomb, some of the soldiers went into the city to report to the chief priests the startling news: they had seen an angel roll away the stone; Jesus had risen from the dead; the tomb was empty, and their mission was over.

Consulting with the elders, the chief priests devised a plan to falsify the resurrection. Presenting a large sum of money to the soldiers, they instructed them, "You are to say, 'His disciples came at night and stole Him away while we slept.' And if this comes to the governor's ears, we will appease

◄ WHEN THE GOING GETS TOUGH ONLY THE TOUGH GETS GOING

him and make you secure. So they took the money and did as they were instructed" (Matthew 28:13-14). Just as Judas exchanged the Savior for silver, the soldiers sold out their peace and testimony for money and honor, even at the point of risking their very lives.

The soldiers and chief priests' conspiracy against righteousness continues to be manifested in the Christian world. Potential witnesses of Christ hide behind traditions and the favor of men rather than preaching the truth they know from the Bible. For instance, they exchange the truth about what happens when you die (the sleep of the dead) for man-made doctrines, and to be known and accepted by the multitudes.

One of the devil's most insidious attacks on the character of God lies in a denial that death is a sleep. To deny the death-sleep understanding is to ignore Biblical declarations about a resurrection event to be staged by heaven (see I Thessalonians 4:16, 17). The experiences of Lazarus and Jesus both underline their emergence from a grave rather than from a trip to heaven. It is difficult to imagine Lazarus being joyful in heaven only to return to a sinful world if in death he had been given residence in heaven. Lazarus had nothing to tell his relatives and friends about his experience in death when he had no participation either in heaven or on earth. And after His resurrection, Jesus clarified to Mary that

◄ 56

He had not yet seen His Father. Could the lure of money and popularity prevent allegiance to a belief that belittles the wonderful truth of the resurrection? (See John 6:39-40 and 1 Cor. 15: 12-58.)

Satan and his Angels

When Satan and his angels heard the sound of the coming angel of the Lord and saw his glory, they disappeared from the tomb, fearful that their judgment had come. Death, Hades, worms, and the Grave were left without Satan, while the soldiers remained "like dead men." After Jesus left the tomb and the holy angel had disappeared, Satan and his angels returned to the tomb, only to find out that Jesus was no longer there. It must have been as if Satan was dreaming! Imagine an ensuing conversation between Satan, Death, Hades and the Grave:

Satan (to Death and the Grave): Where is He? What happened?

Death: I have never held anyone like that man before. My strong grip on Him was broken like ropes of sand. I have no words to describe what happened.

Grave: Yea! It looks like He is the Master of all who have ever died. I couldn't keep Him in my belly for long. That earthquake caused me some serious stomach pains; I had to let Him go out.

Satan: Why didn't you keep Him forever, just as I told you? I thought we agreed to keep Him down there. We have been trying to get Him throughout His ministry and failed; this was our only and last chance. But why did you let Him go? I thought you guys were stronger than He, and together we would keep Him!

Grave (to Satan): But in the midst of all confusion, I looked around and you were nowhere to be found, together with your angels. I never thought that you were such a coward. Where did you hide? You left us here!

Death (to Satan): By the way, Satan, when that man came out of my power, of Hades and of the Grave, He looked more glorious, victorious and confident than anyone who has ever lived or been raised from the dead. He turned and looked back, with a scornful look, and said, "Death is swallowed up in victory. O death, where is your sting? O Hades, where is your victory? I am the First and the Last. I am He who lives, and was dead, and behold, I am alive forevermore. And I have the keys of Hades and Death. Those who die believing in me, I will ransom them from the power of the grave; I will redeem them from death. O Death, I will be your plagues! O Grave, I will be your destruction! Pity is hidden from My eyes" (see 1Corinthians 15:54-55; Revelation 1:17-18; Hosea 13:14).

And since you were not here, Satan, that man took all the keys of Death, of Hades and of the Grave, before we made any copies. This means that for anyone who died or will ever die believing in His name, He will unlock their Graves, Death and Hades, and bring them back to life to live for ever and ever. This troubles me!

Satan: You mean we can't make a new set of locks for the Grave, Death and Hades, even to keep His followers down there forever?

Death, Hades and Grave (shouted back to Satan): He got everything we had, no secrets, no power are left with us.

Grave: If the resurrection of that one man caused me such a pain in my innermost, I don't think I can stand when He comes to call the multitudes back to life!

The Power of the Resurrection

In addition to what we have said so far, let us point out some more key concepts regarding the power of the resurrection.

First, the display of God's power in the resurrection assures us that He can lift us up from the pressures of our circumstances even now, before the ultimate time of the physical resurrection. Paul reports a time in Asia Minor when persecutions were severe, problems arose on every side, to the extent that death seemed imminent. With the pressure almost unbearable for Paul and his companions, they turned their thoughts to the God who raises the dead. Paul declares:

> **8** For we do not want you to be ignorant, brethren, of our trouble which came to us in Asia: that we were burdened beyond measure, above strength, so that we despaired even of life. **9** Yes, we had the sentence of death in ourselves, that we should not trust in ourselves but in God who raises the dead, **10** who delivered us from so great a death, and does deliver us; in whom we trust that He will still deliver *us*" (2 Corinthians 1:8-10).

The resurrection of Christ, therefore, is God's declaration of His power to save us when we become His people, no matter what situations we may encounter. Then, our obstacles, our disappointments, are God's opportunity to show His saving power. We in turn give praise and honor to Him alone. With the God who raises the dead on our side, we have a present help, a strong tower, where we can hide from all the blasts, traps and missiles that the devil and his demons may throw our way. The empty tomb tells us that we can face our tomorrows in His name, in this present life.

Second, though God's Son did not need to go

through suffering to understand our pain, the week-end of the cross, of suffering and the resurrection, tells us that God does not leave us alone during our suffering. He understands our pain and suffer-ing, our trials and the weight of our temptations. When we face suffering and death, He reminds us that these too are temporary. The cross and the empty tomb tell us that the price of our redemption is paid for in full. We can, therefore, continue with the race, because victory has been decided, and the finish line is near.

Lastly, the resurrection of our Lord is an indis-pensable pillar of our faith in the God who is able to save us to the uttermost. Whenever it is time to deliver His people from either slavery of sin, pov-erty, sickness and death or negative circumstances, no conspiracy, no demons or earthly power can stand on His way. Since He died just as He said, and He rose from death just as He said, we can rest assured that He will come again just as He said. His promises are true; He is faithful to keep them.

We can return repeatedly to the resurrection story for insight and assurance of God's presence dur-ing our dark days. One song writer tells how God brought a Sunday experience at a time her soul was wondering if God really cared for her. She says, "It was winter of 1995 and we had prayed and wrestled with God longer than we anticipated. I was over-whelmed by our predicament and began to dwell more on my misfortunes and negatives. The more I thought about my misfortunes, the more I became discouraged and depressed by my situation. Just at the point when I thought there was no reason to trust in God, a small voice talked to me to begin to count my positives in the same manner that I have been counting my negatives. My Friday experience was turned into a Sunday experience! That's when I realized, like the disciples during the weekend when Jesus died, how we easily get swept away by the circumstances of life and completely forget that God is in control of our lives everyday. Then this song came into my mind: 'Learn to Trust in Him'"

I know there are days when I am very low
Sad and losing trust in Him who made me
But I know He is a friend (x2)
Who never changes though I may change

Chorus
Learn to trust in Him
Don't lose faith
He is with you all the time
Learn to trust in Him

There are times when sorrow clouds my life
Then I lose hope in Him who is my Lord
Yet I know yes I know (x2)
He never fails, though I may fail

There are moments when life is tempest tossed
Fearful forget there is wisdom above the storm
But I know there is a rock (x2)
That never shakes, though I may shake [2]

CHAPTER 5

The Just Shall Live by Faith

Habakkuk 2:2-4

2 Then the LORD answered me and said: "Write the vision. And make it plain on tablets, That he may run who reads it.

3 For the vision is yet for an appointed time; But at the end it will speak, and it will not lie. Though it tarries, wait for it; Because it will surely come, It will not tarry.

4 "Behold the proud, His soul is not upright in him; But the just shall live by his faith.

A story went around that three young pastors were caught right in the act of adultery. At that time, these three pastors were working for the same church organization; one was the ministerial secretary, and the second was responsible for the youth ministries, while the third was responsible for the stewardship and evangelism ministries. Three pastors at one go! Could this be! What a tragedy!

The leader of the church organization called

the three pastors at separate times, but in succession, into his office to let them know that he knew what the pastors had done. He said to each one of the pastors, "I know that one can fall and rise up again. I am just telling you as your fellow worker, without any intentions to either investigate the matter or to do anything about it. Don't even tell your wife. If there is a need, I will be the one to tell her. And by the way, the witnesses are many, and they will overwhelm you. Your fellow colleagues (the other two pastors who were also caught in the act) have already confessed to me that they have indeed committed adultery (Ba bangwe ba dumetse)."

The three pastors, individually, said to the leader, "That is not true about me. I am going to tell my wife. I want my case to be investigated and appropriate actions to be taken just as we do to other ordinary church members." Those three guys told their wives. However, for sometime the three pastors did not talk about the issue among themselves, for each one of them thought that the other two were guilty and had confessed before the leader, and that they were not even in favor of investigating the issue. As the leader had meant it to be, each one was suspecting the others, dying as individuals, instead of joining forces to deal with their enemy.

They were each surprised, later on, to realize that they were all making appeals to the executive committee, that their leader told lies when he said "Other pastors have confessed that they have indeed committed adultery." At the executive committee meeting, there was no hearing of the case, for the leader had connived with his teammates to destroy the young men's reputation, and the leader's teammates were the majority. By the way, this was not the first time for this president and his teammates to do this. He had done this to one of the senior pastors, about twelve years before, and at that time they achieved their goal.

The young pastors made their appeals to the higher church organizations; to the union and to the division, respectively, but received no hearing, no justice. Meanwhile the field president and his friends continued to spread the story near and far. On the other hand, the three young pastors and their wives went through emotional pain, prayed and cried to God, by day and by night for God to intervene and bring about justice. The church organizations were silent. God seemed to be silent too!

By the way, there is no problem as long as the Ship of Zion sails on the ocean; a problem arises when water begins to flood the Ship of Zion. This is to say, there is no problem as long as the church of God sails in the world, but there is a problem when the world begins to get into the church, as, for example, when church leaders struggle for power and maintain it at the expense of justice and righteousness. We have a problem whenever we proclaim heaven and peace from the pulpit, and yet offer people hell and fear in our offices, when our church politics result in many being professionally assassinated, whenever we have more victories and shouting at the stadium than we have from the pulpit and from the pews at the church, whenever there are more players than prayers in the church, more services and no converts—then we know that the church is no longer sailing in the world, but the world is getting inside the church.

The church ought to make a difference in the world, preserving it from corruption and lawlessness. The church ought to be a lighthouse in the midst of dark times. Rather than being a place where we meet our fiercest storms, the church should become a hiding place from storms!

Too much religion without spirituality can be deadly. This was the concern of the prophet Habakkuk. He saw violence and corruption in the temple, among the Israelites, in the streets, and by the city gates, where the elders were bribed to deal with cases that were presented to them. The king, the priests, and the false prophets had led the nation of Israel away from God. He saw the strong taking advantage of the weak with no regard for human life. Justice was perverted and power was abused. The leaders had no integrity; evil was regarded as good, and good as evil. The sins of other nations had become the sins of God's people as well: sexual immorality, idolatry, bribery and witchcraft.

Looking at the people of God, Habakkuk asked God, "For how long will you let wickedness prevail in Israel? When will you hear my prayer?" This is an old question, "How long?" It is a question that has been asked throughout the ages, "How long?" Abraham asked "How long will I have to wait for a child?" During their Egyptian bondage, the children of Israel asked "How long are we to wait for our deliverance?" Job, his wife and his friends, wondered, "For how long?" would Job go through that ordeal. In Jerusalem, Jesus asked the Jews, "For how long will I keep on gathering you, like a hen gathering her chicks under her wings, as you keep on getting away from me?" (Matthew 23: 37, paraphrased). For how long would He keep up with their unbelief, their doubts and their stubbornness? And for how long will He have to keep up with our unbelief, our self-centeredness and our inconsistency?

I suggest that "How long?" is not a question of time, but a question of patience, of faith as well. During his wait for a promised child, Abraham's faith wavered; he sought to answer his own prayer; he blessed himself, and Ishmael was born. In Egypt, some Israelites died in faith, not out of faith. Their children were delivered by faith, and yet some became impatient on the way, faithless, while some arrived in the Promised Land by faith. Job provides an almost singular example of faith when under siege. It is said of Job, "In all this Job did not sin with his lips" and "nor charge God with wrong" (Job 2:10; 1: 22). He did not lose his faith, no matter "how long" the trial prevailed.

On the other hand, I would point out that the question of "how long or why?" is not necessarily a question of doubt, faithlessness, fear or weakness, but rather, a human cry whenever pain reaches the core of our being. It is a question that arises from a soul that goes "through the valley of the shadow death" (Psalm 23:4). If we have to cry when facing overwhelming straits, let us cry; but turning back from our faith should not be an option.

In the midst of waiting, in the midst of suspense, when God seems to be silent and unconcerned about our situation, faith in our God of yesterday and the God of our tomorrow becomes a sure anchor for our souls. At times there are a lot of "how longs" and "Why me, Lord?" Faith can become the "substance" (Hebrews 11) that remains. In His darkest moment on the cross, Jesus, who was there because of His redemptive love for lost humanity and His consonance with His father's will, found His faith in His father's providence sustaining Him even as He said, "My God, my God, why have you forsaken me?" (Matthew 27:46).

It would seem that Habakkuk, in the midst

of uncertainties, found himself more concerned about the situation of Israel than God Himself was. The prophet seemed to be moving at the speed of 150km/h while God was doing 50km/h to promote righteousness. We can imagine God addressing the impatient Habakkuk: "Habakkuk, cool down; life is a marathon, so don't burn all your energy in the first miles; we have more miles to cover. Unlike a 100-meter race, our race has curves, turns, mountains and valleys to cover, and it takes time. So, don't get impatient. Another day will rise up, Habakkuk!" (Moruti Habakuke, kana botshelo ga se lobelo lwa gwaragwara. Le potlapotla ke la basimanyana, tonakgolo re baya dinao. Wela dibete, Moruti Habakuke!)

When God finally answered Habakkuk, He didn't meet the prophet's expectations. God announced that the Babylonians would be His instrument of punishment, and would stop the prevailing wickedness in Israel. Quoting from the blessings and curses announced by Moses in Deuteronomy 28, God was reminding Habakkuk of the conditional prophecy regarding Israel's fate, a covenant based on their choices to obey or disobey. In response to their disobedience, God would send a mighty nation to carry them as captives into a foreign land. God had been faithful in His part of the covenant, but the Jews had failed to fulfill their part of the

We can consider faith based upon the word of God to be like receiving a substantial check from a person whom we know to be trustworthy. We can rejoice that we have the money even before cashing the check. In the same way, when we place our faith in God, we can rejoice over His promises before they come to pass, because we know He is trustworthy; His account never runs out of funds/blessings. Faith assures us of the reality of things unseen, as if they are already objects of sight, rather than objects of hope.

covenant. Therefore, their days of peace and ease were numbered. The Babylonians would catch the people with hooks, as though they were fish, dragging them off in nets. Yet the Babylonians would praise their own power, their nets and their gods for their success, rather than acknowledging the God of heaven.

Habakkuk could not reconcile the fact that God, in His holiness and justice, would use the most wicked nation to punish God's people. He posed serious questions to God: "Are you going to let us perish in their hands? How are we going to survive? Are you going to sit back and let our enemies praise their power, their skills and their gods instead of you? How can a wicked nation be God's instrument of correction?" Going to his prophetic office, to his watchtower by the walls of Jerusalem, Habakkuk waited for God to answer his arguments.

Before long God responded (Habakkuk 2:4): "Behold the proud, His soul is not upright in him; But the just shall live by his faith." In other words, God said to Habakkuk, "Don't worry about the righteous, Habakkuk, for they will just live by faith in a foreign land as they have always been living by it at home. Circumstances will not alter the faith of the righteous." Faith in this context, therefore, would be the only means of survival for the exiles. Those who made faith their treasure while in Israel would take their treasure with them to Babylon; their faith would not be stolen or corrupted, nor would it betray them. When homesick, they would live by faith. Faith would be the irreducible minimum required by God to live in the exile.

On the other hand, God declared (Habakkuk 2:9-10) that those who had made violence their treasure while living in Israel would have no means for survival in the far country. All the common resources for their lives would be cut off. Those who had taken advantage of others while living in Israel would be taken advantage of by the Babylonians. The faithless would either come to their senses, remembering God as their provider, or they would live like the Babylonians, without hope.

A life of faithlessness, of pride, of taking advantage of fellow human beings—simply, a life of wickedness, according to God's words in Habakkuk—is a life that has no sustaining power. When disaster strikes—when one loses power and money—a life of cheating and hypocrisy renders the victims nakedness, no protection, guilt and shame. History presents examples of unprincipled people successfully striving in the evil world to become prosperous. Then when evil days ensue, the devil cavalierly abandons his earthly colleagues, while God, on the other hand, promises to be with those who serve Him till the end of time.

Life presents us with the law of the harvest; we reap what we sow. We sow faithfulness, and reap the wonderful faithfulness of God. We sow corruption now, and find that corruption is in our future. No miracles: if we sow corn, we can not reap rice or wheat.

Faith is depending and trusting in God, for who He is, and for what He can do. Faith is a human "yes" to the divine proposals of love. While grace is a divine "hand" of mercy that reaches and holds human beings, faith is a human hand that reaches and holds onto God. The meeting of grace and faith becomes a "love affair." Faith is like an electric cord that connects an iron to the source of power. Once an iron is connected to the source of its power, you can name any material, and it will do its work, it will iron through. Just as a good iron cannot do anything by itself, we cannot iron through (survive) tough times without being connected to the Source of our Power.

We can consider faith based upon the word of God to be like receiving a substantial check from a person whom we know to be trustworthy. We can rejoice that we have the money even before cashing the check. In the same way, when we place our faith in God, we can rejoice over His promises before they come to pass, because we know He is trustworthy; His account never runs out of funds/blessings. Faith assures us of the reality of things unseen, as if they are already objects of sight rather than objects of hope.

Faith is a God-given spiritual muscle that grows stronger as it is used and grows weaker as it is not used. If we expect our faith to be strong when facing trials, we must recognize that it is not practical to prepare for an event during the event. We surely would not prepare for a wedding day by searching for a potential spouse that day. Obviously, the future spouse, the bridal party, the photographer, and the reception accoutrements would be ready for the event before the ceremony would begin. It takes time, it takes budgeting, and it takes people to prepare for a wedding. In a crisis, there is no opportunity to learn how to depend on God. This must be done beforehand. Relying on God is a daily business.

Just as we would spend time with our close friends, talking and sharing with them, and the relationships and interdependence would grow as time would go by, so we would need to spend time with God through reading His word and talking with Him through prayer, so as to be able to call on Him, like a friend, in time of need. And not only should we read the Bible for guidance, inspiration, but also to see how the righteous in biblical times survived the challenges.

In addition, there are Christian books that testify of God's faithfulness throughout human history. Believers in the past, and some during our times, have trusted in God and prevailed during their storms, and recorded their experiences in books, and in Christian music, and left these as treasures to inspire God's people throughout the decades. All these, the Bible, Christian literature and music, are meant to start and maintain a relationship between us and God. A relationship thus built, by the process of time, with all available human and divine resources, many times would be bound for success during challenging times, we would realize that we are never alone, forsaken and regarded useless before His eyes. Even if we were to fall, we would remember what we would have read about our Friend, that He is faithful to forgive, restore and sustain.

There is a healthy way for Christians to respond to challenges, or crises. It comes by saying, "Oh, oh! Has this come to determine what I'm made of? What will it reveal about what I've been nurturing and sowing? Can I use this event to encourage someone else?" It is during crisis that a difference is made between the wheat and the weeds, between those who are serious and those who are not serious with their faith. Tough times reveal who we are, and they bring a spotlight into our spiritual life.

A charming story surrounds the birth of a beloved Christian hymn, "Jesus, Lover of my Soul," summarizing Charles Wesley's experience in Jesus during severely difficult times. Charles Wesley, the brother to John Wesley, one day sat at his desk to brood over his troubles. As he was still naming his problems one after another, a small bird flew in through an open window, hit him on his chest and scrambled under the lapel of his jacket. Charles could feel the little bird's fast-beating heart; he immediately placed his hand over the frightened bird and went to look through the window to see the reason of the bird's flight. He saw a big hawk flying in circles overhead, and he knew that the little bird was seeking for safety.

As Charles Wesley held the frightened bird close to his bosom, he began to think about his own experience, where he could get refuge for his troubled soul. He concluded that he could take the wings of faith to find refuge in God. For it has been well said, "the just shall live by his/her faith." Thus the hymn, "Jesus, Lover of my Soul," came into being.

Jesus, lover of my soul, let me to Thy bosom fly,
While the nearer waters roll, while the tempest still is high.
Hide me, O my Savior, hide, till the storm of life is past;
Safe into the haven guide; O receive my soul at last.

Other refuge have I none, hangs my helpless soul on Thee;
Leave, ah! Leave me not alone, still support and comfort me.
All my trust on Thee is stayed, all my help from Thee I bring;
Cover my defenseless head with the shadow of Thy wing.

Thou, O Christ, art all I want, more than all in Thee I find;
Raise the fallen, cheer the faint, heal the sick, and lead the blind.
Just and holy is Thy Name, I am all unrighteousness;
False and full of sin I am; Thou art full of truth and grace.

Plenteous grace with Thee is found, grace to cover all my sin;
Let the healing streams abound; make and keep me pure within.
Thou of life the fountain art, freely let me take of Thee;
Spring Thou up within my heart; rise to all eternity.[1]

CHAPTER **6**

He Tested Abraham's Faith

Genesis 22

1 Now it came to pass after these things that God tested Abraham, and said to him, "Abraham!" And he said, "Here I am."

2 Then He said, "Take now your son, your only son Isaac, whom you love, and go to the land of Moriah, and offer him there as a burnt offering on one of the mountains of which I shall tell you."

3 So Abraham rose early in the morning and saddled his donkey, and took two of his young men with him, and Isaac his son; and he split the wood for the burnt offering, and arose and went to the place of which God had told him.

4 Then on the third day Abraham lifted his eyes and saw the place afar off.

5 And Abraham said to his young men, "Stay here with the donkey; the lad and I will go yonder and worship, and we will come back to you."

The Genesis 22 story of Abraham highlights a crucial reminder about maintaining a spiritual relationship with God. Here we see Abraham facing a crisis in his personal journey with God. It was a momentous experience that elevated Abraham, the father of the faithful, from his spiritual sons and daughters. It would be difficult to read this story and deny that Abraham is the father of the faithful! In this chapter, we find Abraham challenged to trust God when His will did not make sense. The greatest of all his trials did not originate with his enemies, but with his closet friend, God Himself, who had always been his enabler to face trials. Through Abraham's experience, we can see that faith is like a telescope: it takes us beyond the transitory, beyond the stars, from what is seen to what is unseen. Further, we come to realize that a journey with God need not make sense at all times. A spiritual journey with God is at times unpredictable – God will take us by surprise and to places and heights we never thought He could.

Genesis 22 begins with some rather unusual and blunt phrases, some disturbing statements, which were doubtless meant to arrest Abraham's attention. We will give attention to a sequence of four interactions: (1) "And it came to pass that after these things, (2) God tempted/tested Abraham's faith, (3) Take your son, your only son, Isaac, whom you love, and (4) Take him now and go to the region of Moriah, sacrifice him there as a burnt offering on one of the mountains."

And it came to pass that after these things

It is said that "it came to pass that after these things." We can be sure that God's timing was perfect; He doubtless had been waiting for a golden opportunity to provide an ultimate growth experience for His chosen one. After a long silence between God and Abraham, perhaps since the time when Abraham and God talked about Ishmael and Hagar having to leave Abraham's household, God broke the silence with a strange request. Perhaps it was prefaced by the intimate greetings typical between friends when they meet after a time of being absent. But "after these things," God came with a ready-made agenda for Abraham.

Decades had gone by since Abraham and God decided to be companions for life. By now Abraham had surely developed a perspective of how his companion worked, based on "these things" he had experienced. What could this mean, "After these things?" Which things?

To highlight a few of them, first, Abraham had to leave his own country and follow God's direction, demonstrating his mastery of the lesson that God comes first before earthly treasures, before relatives, and before comfortable environments, and that the best place to be is where God wants us to be, and the best thing to be doing is doing His will.

Second, God miraculously delivered Sarah,

Abraham's wife, from two kings who almost slept with her. The lesson? Abraham learned that God protects His own servants; they do not need to tell lies to protect themselves.

Third, Abraham and Sarah had a child at the time God said they would. The lesson? God's promises will always come to pass; He never lies and He knows the right time.

The fourth of "these things" was God's watch care over the nomadic Abraham as he moved through a strange land, protecting him from his enemies, and prospering his efforts to provide for an expanding entourage. The lessons? God is the provider; He does not lead us to places where His grace will not provide for our daily needs; and both our physical and spiritual needs are important to God. After these instances, and many others, we might conclude that God was presenting a supreme, almost unthinkable, test for Abraham to demonstrate his confidence in God.

On the other hand, "after these things" could mean "after these blunders" God was testing Abraham. It was important for this man, entrusted with a great promise to become the father of God's chosen people, to demonstrate whether he had learned from his past mistakes. Twice Abraham had said Sarah was his sister instead of his wife; fearful that when Pharaoh and Abimelech asked for her hand in marriage that these kings would kill him in order to consummate a marriage with Sarah. Both kings almost took Sarah as their wife because of Abraham's lie. In another instance, Abraham agreed with Sarah to have a child with Hagar, to "help God out." Abraham had lost patience with God's promise of paternity. Ishmael was born out of wedlock; joy was followed by pain when Abraham had to part with Ishmael. Outside God's plan, success could be short lived. Abraham's faith in these instances did not shine as the father of the faithful. After these blunders, God gave Abraham another chance to exercise his faith in a situation where he would be choosing his way or God's way.

God was testing Abraham. Sometimes the make-over test can be more challenging than the first test. In a make-over test we would be expected to do better because it is believed that we have walked over that path before. The pressure of doing better could be higher, from the teachers, from the close ones, and from the eyes of the witnesses who could be watching for what might happen. As the years go by in our spiritual journey with God, we are expected to become more mature, more responsible, more productive, and begin to live above our earlier failures and mistakes. We would not expect to continue to be infants or children in the faith; even the natural laws would not support that. Everything that is born, either physically or spiritually, has to grow; if it doesn't, there could be something abnormal about it. Hence Abraham's test came after many miles had been covered in his spiritual journey.

Further, "after these things" could mean "after God's acts of long-suffering with Abraham," He tested Abraham. In this case, God wanted to display how far and deep the covenant relationship between Abraham and God could go. "After these things" God knew and was confident that what He had started to work out in Abraham's life, faith and obedience, had come to a certain level of maturity. Though Abraham was not an already finished product of God's grace, he was a testimony to the fact that God perfects those He calls. He is the author, sustainer and finisher of our faith.

Therefore, I would suggest that the temptation, or test, was more about God's character in Abraham than about Abraham. In Abraham, God wanted to display His faithfulness, and that is, He would take a person from one level of faith to another, from one level of obedience to another, and from one degree of maturity to another. God's grace does not leave us where He found us.

Through Abraham's faith and obedience, God wanted to display that He prepares the called, He equips the called, and He sanctifies the called. This can happen because we live by His promises to us, rather than by our promises to Him, and by His faithfulness to us, not by our faithfulness toward Him. For if it were otherwise, our relationship with Him would last but for a season. Bless your heart because of His promises and that "Through the LORD's mercies we are not consumed, because His compassions fail not. They are new every morning; great is Your faithfulness." (Lamentations 3:22-23).

God wanted to point out that . . .
Character, holy character, is a product of life's experiences, of the ups and downs, the valleys and mountain top experiences. It takes time to serve God faithfully, and it takes time to build good character.

God wanted to show that . . .
Following God is a full-time profession in which you are at the job 24/7. There are no visiting professors, but only residents. Following God as a profession involves us at our best and worst. It is a journey in our young age and old age, at our wisest and most foolish of times. It is a walk during our hottest and coolest days, during our success and horrible times. In following God, there is no old age, no retirement. There are no lunch breaks, and no excused absents. In this profession, no one can come to work on your behalf. There are no sick leaves and no holidays.

God wanted to demonstrate that . . .

In following God, unlike in other professions, God does not call the strong, but rather, strengthens the called. He does not interview the qualified, but qualifies the called. In this profession, God does not call on our references, but gives us a new reference. He does not hire the faithful, but makes the called faithful. And He does not enlist the beautiful, but washes clean the redeemed.

God Tested/Tempted Abraham

Another disturbing phrase in Genesis 22 says, "God tested Abraham." In one other biblical text, James 1: 13-15, the Bible declares, "Let no one say when he is tempted, 'I am tempted by God'; for God cannot be tempted by evil, nor does He Himself tempt anyone. But each one is tempted when he is drawn away by his own desire and enticed. Then, when desire has conceived, it gives birth to sin, and sin, when it is full-grown, brings forth death."

Then what could the text mean, when it says "God tempted Abraham" (as used in the King James Version of the Bible)? The word "nissah," which is translated "tempt," is now generally used to imply evil intent to lead into evil, unlike its original meaning, "to prove." The word "nissah" appears 36 times in the Hebrew language of the Old Testament. Sometimes it is used to describe a testing of weapons and armor for their strength and quality. At other times the word is used to portray what a person or a nation has gone through during a period of severe trial or difficulty that was brought by another person or nation. In such instances, the word implies a test that calls for endurance, for a person or a nation to be proved beyond doubt that a high standard has been met or achieved. For

> In following God, unlike in other professions, God does not call the strong, but rather, strengthens the called. He does not interview the qualified, but qualifies the called. In this profession, God does not call on our references, but gives us a new reference. He does not hire the faithful, but makes the called faithful. And He does not enlist the beautiful, but washes clean the redeemed.

instance, the word describes the test Daniel and his friends (Daniel chapter 1) endured after pursuing a vegetarian diet for ten days; they were tested to see if they were just as fit as those who had eaten from the king's table.[1]

Other examples of the use of the word "nissah," or "tempt," are: (a) in 1 Kings 10:1, the queen of Sheba came to the king of Israel, Solomon, "to test him with hard questions," with the intent to test him or verify if indeed king Solomon was as wise as it was reported. (b) In Ex. 17:2, 7; Num. 14:22; Isaiah 7:12, "nissah" is translated to mean presumption, when a person tries to compel God to act according to the individual's own proposal. This is testing God, putting Him to the test. (c) In Ex. 16:4; Deut. 8:2, 16; 13:3; 2Chro. 32:31, "nissah" is used whenever God tried, tested, proved a person.[2]

Therefore, in our text, Gen. 22, like in the case of King Hezekiah in 2Chro. 32:31, God tested Abraham and King Hezekiah to see what they were made of, to see their intentions, and to verify the depth of their commitment and love to Him. This was their God-given opportunity to display their very best intentions of their relationship with their God. This was not a temptation enticing them to fall into sin or to reveal weakness; rather, this was meant to display strength, endurance, high quality, and high level of commitment. It was, therefore, another chance, the best chance for Abraham, to let his faith in God's providence shine, no matter what.[3]

We can then, therefore, say that "God tested Abraham's faith" in Him. God put together circumstances that were to prove Abraham's faith and to take Abraham's faith into the next level. God intended to display how strong His relationship with Abraham was, to prove to the devil, and to all the enemies of righteousness, that indeed Abraham was the father of the faithful.

Moreover, this would show us that even though God could be longsuffering with weaknesses, doubts and fears, He would not leave us in one stage. God would work in us according to His sovereign pleasure, to perfect what He started when we first believed in Him. Like a competent teacher, God will move us from one grade to another, not with mere promotions, but with teaching, learning and passing. God will not settle for the minimum; He goes for the best as far as our characters are concerned.

Your Son, Your only Son

In the third disturbing phrase in our text, Gen. 22, God called for Isaac. God said, "Take now your son, your only son Isaac, whom you love." Why this repetition, or emphasis? God knew that only Isaac was with Abraham, and that he loved Isaac so much. In addition, God said, "Take your only son." All those years, since Ishmael left the household, it had been only Isaac at home with Abraham and Sarah. Isaac was the only son, no mistake about it. There was no reference to another son, to Ishmael.

Given a choice between taking Isaac or Ishmael, from the human point of view, it probably would have been easier for Abraham to take Ishmael instead of Isaac. But God said, "Take now your son, your only son Isaac, whom you love."

God knew that Abraham loved Isaac. Everything at that time in Abraham's life had meaning through Isaac. Isaac was the lens through which Abraham saw the fulfillment of God's future promises. Yet, God was emphatic, specific and repetitious.

Abraham had no choice and no power. This trial threatened his very sense of being in control. But make no mistake. Abraham retained freedom to take the son whom he loved or to reject the direction of God.

Take now... and Sacrifice him

In the fourth disturbing phrase in Gen. 22, God says, "And go to the land of Moriah, and offer him there as a burnt offering on one of the mountains which I shall tell you." We will look at the "now" and the "sacrifice" as they impacted Abraham's life.

The phrase contains an imperative, to be followed; and God added a time element in this command: "now." No delays, no but, no room for consulting with Sarah, or even with Isaac, Abraham was to act "now." The command, therefore, needed to be carried out immediately and personally by Abraham. Offering Isaac as a sacrifice was not meant to be a joint venture between Abraham and Sarah. This was Abraham's test, and he was to face it alone.

Of course, as a couple, Abraham and Sarah

had many things in common, including Isaac's well-being. Working together, as a couple or as a group, can bring a sense of belonging and cooperative energy. But at times God calls us to walk a narrow path alone. At times one person may be the only one who hears, sees and understands what needs to be done. Failure to act promptly now could mean that no one would. Procrastination could be the thief of time and the thief of souls and opportunities too!

Lastly, the command was to take Isaac and to go "and offer him there for a burnt offering on one of the mountains which I will tell you." Had Isaac died of sickness or accident, Abraham would have been bowed down with grief. But now he was being asked to take his son's life. Isaac was a star among many stars, the promise of many children, as many as the sand by the seashore, which Abraham would have. How could he take the life of the first fruits of the promised harvest? And how could Abraham thereafter become a faithful witness to the Egyptians, Canaanites and other nations who offered human sacrifices to their gods? And how could he return to report to Isaac's mother what he had done?

Nevertheless, Abraham started the journey, for he had learned that, notwithstanding the puzzlement of God's instructions, it was better to follow Him than to lean on wisdom from man. The journey must have been extraordinarily silent, the father thinking about the sacrifice and its meaning, the son wondering at his father's silence. Perhaps the son considered that this could be his last journey with his aging father.

At night, Abraham could not find rest; he had to talk with God while the boy and the servants were asleep. The devil knocked at the door of his meditation and whispered, "Maybe the voice you heard was not from God. Why don't you quit? After all, this is an impossible task to perform and you will be excused?" On the other hand, Abraham thought that God would say, "It is enough; I have seen your faith; now return home." But God was silent, He had spoken once, and His voice was still ringing in Abraham's ears. Abraham was not mistaken; he was not following a dream, but he was following the voice of his God.

On the third day, Abraham saw a sign, and his mind was made up to obey God's voice no matter what. He instructed his servants to remain at the foot of the mountain, telling them, "Stay here with the donkey; the lad and I will go yonder and worship, and we will come back to you" (Genesis 22:5). For he now believed that after he had done what God directed, then God would raise Isaac from death, and they would then return to the servants (Hebrews 11:17-19). The servants heard Abraham's assurance, "We will go and come back together, my son and I." He uttered no sound of an alarm, no fear.

Even when the son asked, "Where is the lamb of sacrifice?" the father responded, "God will provide for Himself." And God did provide.

There on Mt. Moriah, the Bible says that Abraham saw the day of Jesus Christ beforehand, and he was glad (John 8:56). Thus Abraham had a foretaste of what God the Father would experience when He offered His only Son on mount Calvary. Here, on Mt. Moriah, Isaac became a type of Jesus Christ. Comparing the experiences of Isaac and Jesus, we might find these parallels:

Isaac	Jesus
Son of promise; long waited for	Son of Promise: long waited for
His birth a miracle	His birth a miracle
Only son of Abraham and Sarah	Only Son of God
In him, all nations would be blessed	In Him, all nations would be blessed
First fruit of Sarah's womb, when it was beyond nature	First fruit of the resurrection, came to life when unexpected.
Three days journey for the sacrifice	Three days in the tomb before the resurrection
Heir of his fathers riches	Heir of God's riches and throne

Offered by his father as a sacrifice to the holy God; his father's love to God.	Offered by His Father as a sacrifice for the lost world; God's love for sinners.
Offered outside his city, on Mount Moriah	Offered outside His city, on Mount Calvary
Willing to die, he chose to obey his father; he was physically strong enough to resist, but he did not.	Willing to die, He chose to obey His father; He could call angels for His rescue, but He did not.
Jointly, with his father, it was a pleasure to worship God.	Jointly with His Father, they reconciled the world unto themselves.

Conclusions

I believe that from Abraham's experience there are several gems of truth, or principles, that we can apply to our own walk with God.

First, God would not call us to make sense out of life's vicissitudes, because at times, our senses would not be sensible; they could fail us. We are, rather, called to know the Lord, personally, to such an extent that we would be able to follow Him during instances when we fail to make sense of His directions, and when we fail to understand our own circumstances.

Second, not all of our "troubles" originate with the devil. God will take us by surprise unbeknown to us. In some circumstances we will understand them, the "whys," either at the end of the trials, or when we get to heaven. We need to accept the fact that even holy bread, holy character, is not baked in a cold oven. God puts the recipe together, puts it in the oven, and He knows exactly what temperature is necessary to bake the bread. By the way, God delights in well-baked bread (character), with good aroma and good taste, which would attract even the passers-by. If we knew all about what He could do, then we would be gods, and we would not need Him. Indeed, His ways are not our ways, and His thoughts are above our thoughts. Let God be God!

Third, God provides for His people. He provides us with energy to carry out His will, and provides the means to do His will. Indeed, "God will provide."

Lastly, the best place to be, is where God's will is being done. Sometimes He may call us to do His will upon a mountain or in the valley. Wherever we are called to go, God will be with us; we will not walk alone.

One artist, in song, "All The Way My Savior Leads Me," says we need not doubt God' leading, for He knows the best, and does all things well. The song was written by one who had learned to trust God in trials and times of needs, that God would not bring her to a place in which His name would not be glorified. We are told that the song writer, Fanny Crosby, wrote over 8,000 Christian hymns despite the handicap she struggled with throughout her life. She lost her eyesight at six weeks of age after a medical procedure.

The song came to Fanny as a result of a prayer; she desperately needed some money. According to her custom, Fanny began to pray. A few minutes later, a gentleman came in and offered her some money, the exact amount she needed.[4] Indeed, God provided! As both a songwriter and a woman of faith, Fanny Crosby's life serves as a testimony of God's faithfulness in our Christian journey.

All The Way My Savior Leads Me

All the way my Savior leads me
What have I to ask beside
Can I doubt His tender mercy
Who thru life has been my guide
Heavenly peace, divinest comfort
Here by faith in Him to dwell
For I know whatever befall me
Jesus doeth all things well

All of the way my Savior leads me
Cheers each winding path I tread
Gives me grace for every trial
Feeds me with the living bread
Though my weary steps may falter
And my soul a thirst may be
Gushing from the rock before me
Lo! a spirit of joy I see

And all the way my Savior leads me
Oh the fullness of His love
perfect rest to me is promised
In my Father's house above
When my spirit clothed immortal
Wings its flight to realms of day
This my song thru endless ages
Jesus led me all the way

CHAPTER 7

Do You Also Want to Go Away?

John 6: 66-69
> **66** From that *time* many of His disciples went back and walked with Him no more.
> **67** Then Jesus said to the twelve, "Do you also want to go away?"
> **68** But Simon Peter answered Him, "Lord, to whom shall we go? You have the words of eternal life.
> **69** Also we have come to believe and know that You are the Christ, the Son of the living God."

If we were called upon to judge a marathon race, we could make a mistake by determining the winner even before the race began. We could be easily deceived by the height, muscles and sinews, and by the spectators' shouts as the runners appear on the field. Although tempted to select the person likely to win, we could not be absolutely sure until the race was over. The winner, to be sure, would be someone who persevered. Even if the weather and the road were not desirable, the winner would go on till the end of the race.

On this matter of staying on the track till the end, I believe that quitting should not be an option for the Christian marathon runners. At times God leads us to the race, or to the battlefield of our faith, with other contestants, not that we may be wounded, crushed, or defeated, but that we may win glorious victories which will crown the head of our gracious Leader and Redeemer with many crowns. In addition, our current victories prepare us for future actions of valor as we continue to be on the track.

In our text, John 6:66-69, as many people who were following Jesus began to leave Him, Jesus asked His disciples, "Do you also want to go away?" In other words, His question was, "Will you also quit the race? Will you also abandon the high calling? Will you also become offended because I say and do things in ways you didn't expect, and are you going to leave me too?" This question required a reflec-tive, self–introspective answer, indicating how strong they were to remain on the track. Did they have what it takes to follow Jesus? Pursuing a Christian path takes more than the physical looks, the shouts of the spectators, and the excitement of miracles; it requires stamina, perseverance and a focus on the prize that awaits the saints at the end of the road.

Jesus asked this question, "Will you also go away?" just after He had compared Himself to the physical bread that the multitude had eaten the day before. Jesus declared that people should hunger for Him more than for physical bread. He said if they would eat Him and drink His blood, internalize His words, they would have eternal life. Though they might die, He would raise them at the end of time.

Some followers were offended because His words contradicted their preconceived ideas about what the promised Messiah would be like. As they took offense, many left before the end of the journey, before receiving their prize. They seemed to be content with drinking from their shallow waters, being on the surface of their current religion, uncomfortable with the depths and the realities that Jesus had in store for them. What Jesus offered was different from their traditions and their national pride regarding their favored position among nations. Their spiritual lenses were well established and not subject to challenge.

Many of Jesus' contemporaries were expecting a strong political leader, a Messiah who would deliver them from the Roman oppressors, not to deliver them from sin. Jesus, at least at first, seemed to fit their expectations. He could provide bread and water to His potential army. He could heal the sick and raise the dead in case His soldiers were wounded at the battlefield. However, when He mentioned that He was the real bread, that His words were meant to give life, and that He would raise them up at the end of time, He lost many of the followers. Why? They wanted all their needs to be realized in their current situation. What He said failed to align with their expectations. Therefore, He was not the Messiah; He was not worthy to be followed. They left Him, they stopped running the race, because they believed neither in their leader, in themselves, nor in the prize.

Whenever the Jesus in our minds, in our theology, in our expectations and in our traditions fails to match up with the Jesus who is outside, we are likely to question, take offense and quit. Some of our religious traditions, socializations and teachings have created a Jesus who is either too powerless or too powerful for our circumstances and struggles. Whenever what we traditionally know about Jesus and the Person He reveals Himself to be creates a conflict, our spiritual life becomes incongruent, and we might be tempted to quit. Thus John 6 records the fact that many left and went out to look for an active Messiah, who was ready to conquer and deliver them from their present situations.

Some practical circumstances in our lives can threaten our walk with Jesus. Imagine being raised in the church, falling in love and being married in the church with great expectations, then experiencing the unexpected, wrenching strains of poor marital relationships or divorce. Or imagine earnestly attempting to train our children in the way of the Lord, albeit as imperfect parents, and losing our children to the world. Further, we might at one time have felt the call from God to join the ministry or to work for God in a given capacity, and yet found these positions bringing pain and disappointment. The question is, "Whenever we are disappointed by our Christian spouses, by our children, by our workmates, and even by our fellow Christians, are we going to quit the race? When our expectations about God's presence in our relationships, in raising our children, and in our relationships with one another in the church are not so ideal as we might have wished, can we go on when there are no miracles?"

At this point, we need to consider two things. First is the fact that each one of us has the power of choice. We choose every day, every year, to either follow the Lord or not, to remain in our relationships or not, and to be faithful in everything or in some things. If those we love decide to quit following God, or if they are overcome by evil, will we remain standing with God, if there is no visible miracle? Second, there is the issue of where our prime allegiance resides. Are God's gifts an end in themselves, or a means to praise Him? If His gifts seem to cease, have these become our gods, so that when they go, our faith also goes? Is our following God miracle-centered, gift-centered, or is it just centered on who He is in our lives?

This question, "Do you also want to go away?" is very important, because it seems that it is easier to trust God when everything is at peace, but trusting God becomes a challenge whenever the spiritual formulas that we have learned and used before fail to solve the current life's equations. For instance, sometimes we might pray and claim His promises for healing on behalf of our loved ones and God might seem to take time to answer, or seem not to care until our loved ones die. At the time of our disappointment, as we look around, our neighbors may seem to be untouched by life's vicissitudes, doing well as if God is always on their side. During such times, do we stop following Jesus?

Moreover, it may look as if we have a life of suffering, defeat, toil and snares. We conclude that we were born to be chickens instead of eagles, which can fly above the storms, above the ordinary. When such feelings come, it may look as if we were born to forever inherit the culture of poverty, suffering, and of trying without success, as if God has forgotten our residential addresses. In my language, we speak of this as a seeming bewitchment (E ka re motho o loilwe. Moloi wa teng a bo a swa a ise a direlole motho yoo wa batho! Mo ke senyama sa koko e ntshonyana).

The people, who followed Jesus in the beginning, seemed to be willing to be His disciples no matter what the cost might be. Now, on a particular occasion, we see their true motives. The people wanted sign after sign to keep on following Jesus. For them the equation was simple: no sign, no faith in Jesus; no food and we quit. Their faith could not withstand temporary physical hunger and thirst, and they could not bear long with the stringent requirements of the race, which had elements opposite from their expectations. We have similar responses in our generation; we are becoming more and more miracle-centered, prosperity-centered and impatient. Spiritually motivated patience and endurance, hallmarks of runners in a marathon, are fading away like dew in the morning. Modern faith can degenerate rather like the pursuit of fast food: you just go through the driveway and you have the food. Just order it, and it comes. If it does not come, go to another restaurant!

On the other hand, however, we need to note that Jesus did not say it was wrong to supply physical bread. After all, He was the one who had fed the crowd yesterday; He still supplies our daily bread. In addition, He was not ignorant of the fact that His followers were oppressed, abused, and in need of freedom from the Romans. Oppression, racism, slavery, evil, as it manifests itself in different forms and colors, many times robs us of peace within, peace that only Jesus can give, and stands like a veil between us and the Master, who cares about our well-being. In the midst of all these trades of unfairness, our faithfulness on the track should not be dependent on what does or does not happen to others around us, or in the socio-political conditions of this planet. Waiting for the disappearance of the Romans and for a change in the socio-political world might delay our present joy in having a relationship with Jesus for who He is; focusing on what He is not doing about the Romans could deter our progress with Him. We should be aware that His longsuffering and mercies can extend to the Romans and to non-believers whom we currently find to be difficult.

In a world littered with pigments of broken promises, shattered with unfulfilled dreams, we are either going to go on with Jesus, or quit the race to seek answers from the rabbis of the day. If we are to go on, Christianity should provide us with a bush-guard (a protective metal device attached in front of vehicles) which we can use to deal with all the darts that come our way. With the bush-guard of His word that gives strength from day to day, we should be able to collide with life, like two vehicles involved in an accident, and remain standing. Our marathon race might take us through the valleys, up on the mountaintops, and through dangers and snares, but we are never alone, even when the going is tough, and even when it does not look as if He is watching over us.

We may not be healed from our physical ailments, but we may experience spiritual healing and become resurrected from our spiritual deformities. Let us be aware that sometimes the minority might not become the majority, the powerless might not become the powerful, the low might not become the high, and the called ones might become the rejected ones. Thus, if we were to lose heaven, we would be losing twice: losing this world and its comforts, and losing the world to come and its wonders. Therefore, if we are to lose anything, it should be only this world and its comforts, but not the world to come and its wonderful relationships. For in the world to come, our place is secure, and our voices, with those of many others, will be heard before the throne of the monarch of the entire universe. Even though we may not be rich and prosperous with earthly goods, yet if we feed from the spiritual bread from heaven, Jesus our Lord, we can face sickness, death, hunger, and whatever tribulations we might be called to endure, with a peaceful mind, with a positive attitude.

We may not be healed from our physical ailments, but we may experience spiritual healing and become resurrected from our spiritual deformities. Let us be aware that sometimes the minority might not become the majority, the powerless might not become the powerful, the low might not become the high, and the called ones might become the rejected ones. Thus, if we were to lose heaven, we would be losing twice: losing this world and its comforts, and losing the world to come and its wonders.

We have the disciples' beautifully exemplary answer to the question, "Do you also want to go away?" It was Peter, the impetuous one, who answered for all the disciples with one of the most thoughtful answers they ever gave: "Lord, to whom shall we go? You have the words of eternal life. Also, we have come to believe and know that you are the Christ, the Son of the living God" (John 6:68-69). What confidence! "Do you also want to go away?" and the answer, "No, Lord, we have no other hiding place; we are here to stay. There is no place more desirable to us than going on a journey with you. There is no restaurant that we know of that cooks bread as you do; we remain here and feed upon you till we want no more. Your motel is the most comfortable; you make us feel at home, even before we get there, and our cup overflows. Where else can we go? In you we have found a fountain; none other has ever refreshed us like this. Where else can we go?" What confidence, and what a commitment!

This question still remains, "Do you also want to go away?" As for the disciples, they testify that "we believe and are sure that you are the Christ, the Son of the living God." They have personally tasted the Lord and found Him to be good. Now, they are sure that this is the Christ, the anointed One, the Son of the living God. We can respond as did the disciples on a personal, deep, and confident level.

We can be sure of in whom we have believed; confident of the race we have enlisted ourselves in, having detected all counterfeits as they fall by the wayside before the finish line.

Christianity places its followers in an active role—pursuing a race to the finish. The wonderful news from heaven is that we have a sure example to follow. When Jesus confronts us, "Do you also want to go away?" we can join the hymn writer, James Lawson Elginburg, who worded a firm answer: "I Will Follow Thee, My Savior." From his personal experience, we believe that James had learned that the race can have some turns, thorns, tribulations, afflictions and billows. Nevertheless, James says we follow Jesus because He has shed His blood for us, that He understands every steep of the race, and because our Savior endured similar difficulties that we do, and learned to obey God in all circumstances of life.[1]

I Will Follow Thee

I will follow Thee, my Savior,
Wheresoe'er my lot may be.
Where thou goest I will follow;
Yes, my Lord, I'll follow Thee.

Refrain
I will follow Thee, my Saviour,
Thou didst shed Thy blood for me;

And though all men should forsake Thee;
By Thy grace I'll follow Thee.

Though the road be rough and thorny,
Trackless as the foaming sea,
Thou hast trod this way before me,
And I'll gladly follow Thee.

Though I meet with tribulations,
Sorely tempted though I be;
I remember Thou wast tempted,
And rejoice to follow Thee.

Though Thou leadest me through affliction,
Poor, forsaken though I be;
Thou wast destitute, afflicted,
And I only follow Thee.

Though to Jordan's rolling billows,
Cold and deep, Thou leadest me,
Thou hast crossed the waves before me,
And I still will follow Thee.

CHAPTER **8**

Jehoshaphat and His Enemies

2 Chronicles 20

1 It happened after this *that* the people of Moab with the people of Ammon, and *others* with them besides the Ammonites, came to battle against Jehoshaphat.

2 Then some came and told Jehoshaphat, saying, "A great multitude is coming against you from beyond the sea, from Syria; and they are in Hazazon Tamar" (which is En Gedi).

3 And Jehoshaphat feared, and set himself to seek the LORD, and proclaimed a fast throughout all Judah.

6 and said: "O LORD God of our fathers, *are* You not God in heaven, and do You *not* rule over all the kingdoms of the nations, and in Your hand *is there not* power and might, so that no one is able to withstand You?

21 And when he had consulted with the people, he appointed those who should sing to the LORD, and who should praise the beauty of holiness, as they went out before the army and were saying: "Praise the LORD, For His mercy *endures* forever."

22 Now when they began to sing and to praise, the LORD set ambushes against the people of Ammon, Moab, and Mount Seir, who had come against Judah; and they were defeated.

When Jehoshaphat became king of Judah, the southern kingdom of the people of Israel, after his father Asa (2Chronicles 17), he was confronted by an enemy challenge. The setting for this confrontation bears examination. After the death of King Solomon, the nation of Israel had broken up into the southern and northern kingdoms. The southern kingdom, primarily constituting the tribes of Judah and Benjamin, was referred to as Judah, the Kingdom of Judah, or the People of Judah.

The division of the kingdom of Israel had resulted when King Solomon's son, Rehoboam, took over the throne of David, and threatened to be harsher than his father had been, causing a division among the Israelites, some of whom followed Jeroboam, who became king of the northern kingdom, Israel. Rehoboam remained on the throne in the southern kingdom. After his death, in succession, his son, grandson, and great grandson reigned as kings of Judah. When Rehoboam's great grandson, Jehoshaphat, became king, Ahab was the king of Israel, the northern kingdom (2Chronicles 17 & 18).

Although a strong army, strong security walls, and watchmen on the walls looked impressive, they could not keep an enemy away. Fasting and prayer proved to be more powerful weapons for saving the nation. In our contemporary world, while it is good to have a strong bank account, beautiful houses, solid academic foundation and a good employment record, only God can keep families, marriages and nations together, and at peace. Without God in the equation, all these commodities are like machines without oil. It is God who provides the oil that runs the human machines to provide security and safety.

From his early years of leadership, the Bible states that Jehoshaphat walked in the ways of the God of David his ancestor, and in everything he did, he consulted with God, unlike King Ahab of Israel, who consulted the foreign gods of Canaan. As a result, his kingdom was blessed, and many people from Israel continued to join Judah as they saw how blessed Jehoshaphat was (2Chronicles 16, 17, and 19).

Under his well established kingdom, all Judah brought gifts to Jehoshaphat, so that he had great wealth and honor; his soldiers multiplied, from four hundred thousand to over a million in Jerusalem, in addition to those in other cities; he conquered more cities, gained more subjects; neighboring nations feared to attack him; reigning in peace, he destroyed places where idol worship had been established. His kingdom was God-centered. In addition, Jehoshaphat called for reformation among his leaders and followers, directing them to judge carefully, without injustice, partiality or bribery (2Chronicles 16, 17, and 19).

However, in the midst of peace and prosperity, while surrounding nations feared Jehoshaphat and his God, three nations—Ammon, Moab and Mount Seir—joined their armies and the powers of their gods against the people of Judah. These enemies of God's people reasoned that once their armies and their gods were combined, no army or god, even Jehoshaphat and Jehovah, could withstand their forces. As they headed for Jerusalem, messengers warned Jehoshaphat that a vast army was on its way to his kingdom (2Chronicles 20:2).

How would Jehoshaphat and Judah deal with this crisis? First, Jehoshaphat took his fears to the Lord. Yes, Jehoshaphat was afraid. He did not know what to do. The situation was beyond his natural capabilities and he needed a supernatural power to go through such a crisis. Providentially, Jehoshaphat, like his forefathers, had learned to take his fears to the Lord. His faith in the God of his fathers was contagious. Caught up in his faith, the people followed the example of their leader in seeking God's guidance. Like the Ninevites at the time of Jonah, both the leaders and followers humbled themselves before the God of heaven. Relying neither on their great army or weapons of war, past victories or wisdom, Jehoshaphat asked for God's direction and for the outcome of the war.

Throughout the kingdom of Judah, there was fasting and praying. Men, women, and their children ignored the desires of their flesh; they denied themselves of tasty food and drink, and emptied themselves of sin and selfishness as they searched for God's will. The voice of God was stronger than the voice of their circumstances which said, "The situation is bad, and you are going down." God's grace was stronger than their love for evil. The desire to know God's will was stronger than reliance on their army, on self, on fortified walls, and on their guards.

Although a strong army, strong security walls, and watchmen on the walls looked impressive, they could not keep an enemy away. Fasting and prayer proved to be more powerful weapons for saving the nation. In our contemporary world, while it is good to have a strong bank account, beautiful houses, solid academic foundation, and a good employment record, only God can keep families, marriages and nations together, and at peace.

Without God in the equation, all these commodities are like machines without oil. It is God who provides the oil that runs the human machines to provide security and safety.

In the distractions of a disaster, we can be tempted to rely on what we have, on the experts, and on what we are, rather than putting the Lord into the equation. It seems easier to make a phone call, write a check, and even call people for a demonstration, than to fast and pray whenever we meet moral, financial, political, and family problems. Although it was prudent of Jehoshaphat to provide for a strong army and good weapons of war, their usefulness and effectiveness were born out of fasting and praying. God uses human agencies, resources and abilities, but those who operate these would do well to be God-anointed through payer and fasting.

In addition, it looks as if even when we are faithful to God, we could face multiplying difficulties which tempt us to ask, "If God is leading us, why all these problems? If God has called me to do this, or to be here, why am I in trouble?" These could be very important questions because the three enemy nations were not attacking Israel, the rebellious, but they were attacking Judah, the faithful. It was Job, the righteous, who suffered the most in the hands of the devil, not the sinful, who might have had reasons to deserve boils and misfortunes.

From the experience of Jehoshaphat, these questions, "Why me Lord?" and "Why am I here?" are best answered through fasting and praying.

We can also learn from Jehoshaphat that he knew his spiritual inheritance; he knew how to talk to God, how to "cry to God" and how to prevail. He talked like a child who was born in the family of God and had the right to "cry out" and to be heard. Indeed he was an Israelite, son of Abraham, from the chosen nation, a nation of destiny, from which the Savior of the world would be born. He was a son of David, from the chosen house of the kings of Israel. And above all, Jehoshaphat had a personal relationship with God that could not be doubted. Trusting and obeying the God of his fathers, he could come humbly and yet boldly and confidently before his creator in times of need.

Jehoshaphat successfully identified with the spiritual history of Israel with God: how God delivered Israel, preserved them in their sojourn in the wilderness, and protected them from the nations as they traveled toward the Promised Land. For King Jehoshaphat, these were not just stories, but practical experiences that could be repeated in the lives of God's people throughout the centuries. Hence, in his prayer, Jehoshaphat talks about God's past deliverances, His power, His guidance, and the way He has kept Israel according to His promises. He spoke from his experience and from his position as a child of God, as part of God's movement. Though humble, he was bold, courageous, unstoppable, and lingered long before God's presence as if that was the only way to go about the matter.

Because when we join the family of God, we are given the right to become His children (John 1:12-13), we also are heirs of God's promises and His kingdom with Christ (Romans 8:14-17). As King Jehoshaphat did, we can come before God from a position of power; as sons and daughters within God's kingdom. We have the right to talk to our creator as our heavenly Father, through the name of Jesus and His merits.

Identifying with the community of Christ's family, our spirit of fear and cowardice can disappear as we consult with God, in the name of Jesus, according to our spiritual inheritance in Him. Our past, even when we knew Him not, our present and our future are all packaged in the life of Jesus Christ. In Jesus, we are the right people, the right nation; we are at the right place, we are the majority, where we can "cry to God" and be heard.

From the experience of Jehoshaphat, we can learn the importance of magnifying the name of the God of heaven. Though he was the king of Judah, Jehoshaphat recognized that the God of heaven reigns over all the earthly kingdoms, as King of kings and Lord of lords. God is the creator and sustainer of His creation. Exerting power over all,

God oversees the rise and fall of kings; none can resist His power (Daniel 5:21).

Acknowledging that God is all powerful and all present, and that nothing is beyond His reach, Jehoshaphat found his enemies and their gods diminished in his mind. To acknowledge God's supremacy in times of need helps us put things in the right perspective, aware that He who is for us is greater than whoever is against us. Lifting up God in His sovereignty places us where we're supposed to be, mortal and dependent on Him.

In another exemplary move, Jehoshaphat's army recruitment process focused not on the strength of the men, but on men who could sing praises to God. They did not sing songs of petition, but songs of praise, giving honor to the Lord for who He is, for "the beauty of Holiness" and for His everlasting love (verse 21). The Bible reports, "Now when they began to sing and to praise," (verse 22), God caused confusion among their enemies; their enemies killed one another.

Jehoshaphat and his army could sing songs of praise because they had appropriated God's promises into their lives. In response, God sent a promise that the victory was theirs. They believed the word of God, praising Him even before they saw the victory.

The word of the Lord made them see what God saw, all their enemies already dead. In essence, they saw all this before it happened, because God had promised it. And as they marched, their eyes did not depart from seeing the beauty of the Lord. Hence, they could not do otherwise except to praise Him, blessing His wonderful name.

The psalmist has instructed us (Psalm 100: 4-5) to "Enter into His gates with thanksgiving, and into His courts with praise. Be thankful to Him, and bless His name. For the Lord is good; and His mercy is everlasting, and His truth endures to all generations." Perhaps our murmuring, complaining, and sadness, after our prayers and reading the word God, would be a sign that we have not entered "His gates," that we have not appropriated His word, believing it and seeing the beauty of His holiness. God's wonderful miracles for Jehoshaphat's army occurred when they were praising Him in the wilderness, rather than when they were praying and fasting in the church. Reading His word, fasting and praying should be followed by praise, even before we see what the Lord has prepared for us.

Praising the Lord for who He is, for what He has done in the past, and for what He is going to do, even before we see the results, is part of a prevailing prayer. Praising the Lord is an important piece of the strategy of dealing with our earthly problems. In dealing with whatever problems, we would do well to learn to have time to praise the Lord. God loves praises, and lives in the environment of praises

(Isaiah 6). After all, is He not worthy of our praises? When our minds are filled with our cares, we need to take God at His word, claiming His promises as a "done deal." There's no point in marching to the heavenly Zion without hope and energy.

We can also learn from Jehoshaphat's words of faith, hope and courage, that fear can be dealt with. What we are, what we believe, and what we cherish in our hearts, is revealed in our actions and words, which in turn has an impact on those who are around us. Jehoshaphat's faith, hope and courage shone in his actions and words, galvanizing the people of his kingdom. Review the record: he took his fears to the Lord in prayer; his people followed his leading; he bowed before the Lord to worship when the answer was given; all the people of Judah fell down in worship; he encouraged his army to trust in the Lord and to believe His prophets for their own success and prosperity; the musicians started to praise the Lord. He did not talk about his fears, or act on his doubts; these would have paralyzed the rest of his army, instead of inspiring faith in his army. His faith, hope and courage were irresistibly contagious, and left no alternative way out of the situation.

Finally, Jehoshaphat marched to the battlefield, instead of merely waiting in Jerusalem for a miracle. He did not go out to help the Lord for what He had already done. He went out to collect the spoils of the victory. The battle was fought and won in the closet (in the prayer room), and the spoils were collected on the battlefield. We can conclude that our battles are to be well fought and won in our wrestling with God; then we will be able to march out with courage to the battlefield (into the world of activities) to realize our promised victories over our troubles.

From the experience of King Jehoshaphat, we learn that we will deal with our enemies, temptations and problems better if we develop the art of talking and listening to God. In our prayers we should carry the spirit of praise and thankfulness, of magnifying the name of the Lord, bringing along our faith, hope and courage. All these factors are based upon the fact that we are sons and daughters of God; we have a solid spiritual inheritance through His Son Jesus Christ. Therefore, the magnetism of God's love and His faithfulness should always be stronger than our circumstances.

King Jehoshaphat, as stated by King David before him, reminds us that "the LORD also will be a refuge for the oppressed, a refuge in times of trouble," and that "God is our refuge and strength, a very present help in time of trouble" (Psalm 9:9; 46:1). One artist puts these two texts (Psalm 9:9 and 46:1) into a wonderful piece, "God is our Shelter," which reminds us that we can call on God in times of trouble, and like King Jehoshaphat, and

God will hear our prayers, and we will praise His name.

God is our Shelter

God is our shelter and our friend
He is always ready to help in times of trouble

Chorus
He says call on me in times of trouble
I will hear your voice
I will save you and you will praise my name

Are you heavy laden, are you weak or feeble
Just look up and praise His name

Behold! Behold! Behold God at the Door ....[1]

CHAPTER 9

Challenges Are Like a Quarry

1 Kings Chapters 5 & 6; 1 Peter 2

1 Kings 6:7

7 And the temple, when it was being built, was built with stone finished at the quarry, so that no hammer or chisel or any iron tool was heard in the temple while it was being built.

1 Peter 2:5

5 you also, as living stones, are being built up a spiritual house, a holy priesthood, to offer up spiritual sacrifices acceptable to God through Jesus Christ.
6 Therefore it is also contained in the Scripture, "Behold, I lay in Zion A chief cornerstone, elect, precious, And he who believes on Him will by no means be put to shame."

Both the Old and New Testaments talk about God's building, a holy temple. In the Old Testament, God's temple was built by King Solomon, the son of David; the builders used stones, timber, gold and other expensive materials. These stones and other building materials were prepared, polished, cut and shaped before they were brought to the building site. In the New Testament, the building materials for God's temple are believers, the living stones, with Jesus as the cornerstone of the building. In the Old Testament building, King Solomon used his chosen men as agents of the cutting, shaping and polishing of the materials, whereas in the New Testament God allows circumstances to be His agents of the preparation.

The Scriptures (1 Kings 5 to 6), tell us that "it took seven years to build the temple" (6: 38). Solomon wanted a strong structure that would withstand the test of time, storms, and all kinds of weather changes. Time, energy, human skills, and strong building materials were to be invested in the building. Another lofty purpose guided them; they wanted to show their children and the heathen world, throughout the coming generations, that their supreme, particular, most beautiful and holy God was deserving of a costly temple for His dwelling. Hence, costly materials and skilful artists were used, and laborers were specifically assigned to take part in the building. There was no haphazard work, for it was to represent the God who redeemed and saved them.

In addition, the Bible says, "And the temple, when it was being built, was built with stone finished at the quarry, so that no hammer or chisel or any iron tool was heard in the temple while it was being built" (1 Kings 6:7). What needed to be cut was cut, shaped and polished before it was brought into the building site at Jerusalem. An atmosphere of sacredness prevailed there, with no noise of building tools present. The stones that were to be the building blocks were cut and shaped at the quarry. Their dimensions and fittings were determined at the quarry outside Jerusalem. This was to be a unique structure, unlike any other building in the nation and outside Israel.

A parallel structure is described in the New Testament, God's current temple is being built using living stones, the believers, with Jesus as the cornerstone of the building. God now dwells in a living structure, a building that has eyes, ears and feet, a living structure that has members with different spiritual gifts, ready to do ministry as holy priests. The problems and challenges that believers are to go through are the quarry that prepares them to fit into the holy building. Like the Old Testament temple, the New Testament temple is meant to withstand the test of time, entering even into eternity. The temple is to stand trials, temptations, disappointments, ridicule, suffering and persecutions, which constitute the storms and the weather conditions of the New Testament temple.

Moreover, like the Old Testament building, the new one is built with costly materials; Jesus, the Son of God, is the cornerstone, and the believers, bought with

His precious blood, are the building blocks. Though salvation is a free gift to sinners, it has been paid for at a high price, the blood of the Son of God. Just like in the Old Testament building, where the stones were selected, prepared and set aside for the holy use, in the New Testament, the living stones are selected, prepared and set aside for the building. Called from the ordinary and then polished, we become part of the building not only through His word and blood, but also through trials and temptations. Life on earth, with trials and challenges, is like a quarry where precious stones are mined, cut and prepared for a special purpose. And God does not waste time and effort in mining and polishing base elements; He goes for the marble, the gold and the diamonds.

It took time, energy and expensive materials to build the Old Testament temple, and it takes God's time, effort and precious stones to build the New Testament temple. Holy character is not a result of a haphazard work, and it does not come overnight, but is a work of a lifetime. Though it might take a moment to be selected (saved), it takes time and effort to build a holy character and maturity. The chiseling, hammering, cutting of the unwanted edges and polishing of the rough surfaces is done in this quarry, our world of sin, for in the New Jerusalem there will be no sound of any building instrument. The work in the quarry has to be done and completed outside the New Jerusalem. God molds those who are ready to be molded, and prepares those who have the courage and the will to let Him do so.

Life's challenges, therefore, are like the building tools that are meant to shape up the building blocks. The hammer, the chisel and the axe are not meant to destroy, but to cut the corners, smooth the sharp edges, and prepare the building blocks, to fit them for a higher service. God is building a unique structure, comparable to none. All the defects that we have because of sin must go, but this is not an easy process. There will be tears and painful moments, for the quarry polishing is now being applied to living stones. And after we have been tested and

---

Life's challenges, therefore, are like the building tools that are meant to shape up the building blocks. The hammer, the chisel and the axe are not meant to destroy, but to cut the corners, smooth the sharp edges, and prepare the building blocks, to fit them for a higher service. God is building a unique structure, comparable to none. All the defects that we have because of sin must go, but this is not an easy process. There will be tears and painful moments, for the quarry polishing is now being applied to living stones. And after we have been tested and tried like Job, the Lord knows that we will come forth as pure gold (Job 23:10).

tried like Job, the Lord knows that we will come forth as pure gold (Job 23:10).

It is a paradox in the Christian life that the process of the quarry, problems in life, is to bring the best out of us. History reminds us repeatedly that martyrs, thrown to their death in the lions' den, have died testifying of the Lord's greatness. Though they were assaulted and ridiculed, they found comfort in the midst of their sufferings, and they have blessed others in the process. Devastated by hatefulness or sometimes by incurable diseases, they learned to trust in God rather than in men and their circumstances of the time. As they faced death with faith, their attitude unshaken, many who observed their constancy were encouraged to follow their example, even becoming martyrs themselves.

Some of Christendom's most comforting hymns have been written by men and women who found peace in the midst of their storms. Thomas Dorsey wrote, "Precious Lord, Take My Hand" after he had lost his wife and child; Charles Wesley wrote, "Jesus, lover of my soul, let me to thy bosom fly" when he had reached the bottom, and Horatio Spafford wrote "It is well with my soul" after he had lost his financial investments, and his children were swallowed and buried by the ocean. Truly, trials and problems at times can be a platform on which the faith of the saints shines brightest, and on which God's sustaining power is manifested!

Further, trials, the quarry processes, have a way of highlighting our weaknesses, insecurities, strengths, and our dependence upon God. They also highlight God's mercy, providence and loving care in our lives. Nothing else compares to trials when it comes to vindicating God's name and the character of His servants whenever His children make it through in the midst of hardships. Interestingly, trials at times highlight the spiritual warfare that is going on; the battle for our souls, between the forces of good and evil. The story of Job is a good example of how, unbeknown to us, God and Satan contend for our allegiance.

On the other hand, we need to note that difficulties not only purify and sharpen the characters of professing Christians, but also those of politicians, social reformers, men and women and boys and girls who dare to stand for principle. We have legacies of men and women of integrity, whose faithfulness to principle was made to shine during their testing times, when the going was tough. If we dare to stand firm for a conviction, knowing that our position may be inviting trouble, and if we continue to stand in spite of whatever might come, we signify that we mean business. Life comes with its turns and curves, with highs and lows, demanding stamina and endurance as we support noble objectives. Thus we support the temple of God, ravaged though it might be by life's storms. Those who remain firm in this New Testament building need never regret it.

On the other hand, unfortunately, some find trials nearly overwhelming—and fail to become what God wanted them to be. They may conclude that the prayer, "And lead us not into temptation, but deliver us from the evil one," is not answered for them. They are tempted to lose their faith, growing tired and crumbling under pressure, while others murmur and complain. To such ones, the call from the everlasting Redeemer remains, "Bring your broken pieces back to the Lord; whenever you grow tired in your destined spot, He does not get tired of you." Another group, when the storm is over, after the Lord has sustained them when their foundations shook perilously, seem to forget their place in the structure. Once fitted into an alcove devoted to peace, they weaken in their positions of supposed power and success, marring the efficiency of the entire building. Thus tyranny rises, wounding the weak and robbing the structure of tranquility.

Researchers posit that when we face a stressful event and feel that we lack control over the outcome, religion may hold out the ultimate control through God's intervention. Knowing that God cares, no matter what may happen, even when we have no better explanation of our pain and suffering, adds meaning to our sometimes meaningless life on planet earth.[1] Only God can give us deeper insight into the source of pain and suffering; the presence of Satan and sin, our pivotal choices, and His ultimate providence, turning all events (good and bad) for the good of them who love Him.

Scholars dealing with terminal illnesses, disabilities and life's challenges, have found correlation between one's coping strategy, negative or positive, and the resulting mental state. Overall, wherever churches and members provided positive social support, individuals coped better and were more adept at facing the unknown with hope, peace and courage than were those who did not believe in God. On the other hand, those who did not know God before the illness exhibited better coping skills than did the negative Christians. Attitudes, either positive or negative during hardships, become even more serious when one suffers from chronic illness such as AIDS/HIV, which may have some kind of stigma, as compared to cancer and diabetes. Also, the way suffering is viewed by Christians can affect their coping with life's challenges. In all situations, either good or bad, our attitude appears to be the most important element that will determine our state of mind.[2]

Translated into Christian understanding, this would mean that our attitude and perception of God during the hard times influence our mental well-being in facing the unknown. If we have positive family and church experiences, we are likely to cope more successfully than do those who have become negative, or who have experienced judgmental statements and attitudes from relatives and fellow church members. It is unfortunate that at times non-believers would cope better than believers with negative attitudes during trials! One author states this well by saying that:

> "This many shock you, but I believe the single most significant decision I can make on a day-to-day basis is my choice of attitude. It is more important than my past, my education, my bankroll, my success or failures, fame or pain, what other people think of me or say about me, my circumstances, or position. Attitude is that "single string" that keeps me going or cripples my progress. It alone fuels my fire or assaults my hope. When my attitudes are right, there's no barrier too high, no valley too deep, no dream too extreme, no challenge too great for me. Yet, we must admit that we spend more time concentrating and fretting over the strings that snap, dangle, and pop – the things that can't be changed – than we do giving attention to the one that remains, our choice of attitude."[3]

The song writer, Horatio Spafford, exhibits a resilient attitude in the words of his song which asserts: "It is well, with my soul" in all circumstances of this life. This hymn was written after two major traumas in Spafford's life. The first was the great Chicago Fire of October 1871, which ruined him financially (he had been a wealthy businessman). Shortly after, while crossing the Atlantic Ocean, all four of Spafford's daughters died when the ship they were in collided with another ship. Spafford's wife, Anna, survived and sent him the now famous telegram, "Saved alone." Several weeks later, as Spafford's own ship passed near the spot where his daughters died, the Holy Spirit inspired these words. They speak to the eternal hope that all believers have, no matter what pain and grief befall them on earth.[4]

When peace, like a river, attendeth my way,
When sorrows like sea billows roll;
Whatever my lot, Thou has taught me to say,
It is well, it is well, with my soul.

Refrain
It is well, with my soul,
It is well, with my soul,
It is well, it is well, with my soul.

Though Satan should buffet, though trials should come,
Let this blest assurance control,
That Christ has regarded my helpless estate,
And hath shed His own blood for my soul.

And Lord, haste the day when my faith shall be sight,
The clouds be rolled back as a scroll;
The trump shall resound, and the Lord shall descend,
Even so, it is well with my soul.

CHAPTER 10

No More Sea

Revelation 21: 1-8

1 Now I saw a new heaven and a new earth, for the first heaven and the first earth had passed away. Also there was no more sea.

2 Then I, John, saw the holy city, New Jerusalem, coming down out of heaven from God, prepared as a bride adorned for her husband.

3 And I heard a loud voice from heaven saying, "Behold, the tabernacle of God *is* with men, and He will dwell with them, and they shall be His people. God Himself will be with them *and be* their God

4 And God will wipe away every tear from their eyes; there shall be no more death, nor sorrow, nor crying. There shall be no more pain, for the former things have passed away."

5 Then He who sat on the throne said, "Behold, I make all things new." And He said to me, "Write, for these words are true and faithful."

6 And He said to me, "It is done! I am the Alpha and the Omega, the Beginning and the End. I will give of the fountain of the water of life freely to him who thirsts.

7 He who overcomes shall inherit all things, and I will be his God and he shall be My son.

8 But the cowardly, unbelieving, abominable, murderers, sexually immoral, sorcerers, idolaters, and all liars shall have their part in the lake which burns with fire and brimstone, which is the second death."

A young man, let us call him Jonathan, went to a school library to look for a book to read over the weekend. He liked novels that have heroes who go out to conquer and destroy enemies. After going through some shelves, his attention was arrested by a promising title. Looking through the introduction, he was convinced that that would be the book for the weekend.

After reading the first three chapters of the book during school study hour, Jonathan had very mild interest about continuing to read. The first chapter introduced the hero as someone who was preparing to win an encounter with an enemy. As he read chapters two and three, the enemy was already having the upper hand; this was not what Jonathan had expected. About to put the book aside with some discouragement, Jonathan followed an impulse to read the last two chapters of the book. At the end, the hero was the conqueror, and the enemy was destroyed. Jonathan now wanted to go back and read the rest of the book. He wanted to know what happened between the beginning and the end.

After dinner Jonathan went to his bedroom, laid down on his bed and returned to the fourth chapter. The enemy was still around, destroying what was good, and giving the hero a hard time. As he read, Jonathan started to talk to himself, "You don't know what I know. I wish you knew what I know." The further he read the book, the louder he shouted, "You don't know what I know. I wish you knew what I know." Jonathan's father, who was reading a newspaper in the living room, heard Jonathan shouting. The father wondered, "I thought my son was alone. Is he going crazy? Did I miss the arrival of his friend?"

Knocking at his son's bedroom door, the father was surprised to find his son alone. He asked Jonathan, "Son, what's going on? Whom are you talking to? What do you know, and who doesn't know what you know?" Jonathan replied, "Dad, this book is about two great champions. This other guy is giving my man a hard time. But I read the last two chapters, and I know how it will end. My man will destroy the enemy. The enemy does not know what I know, that he will at last be defeated by my man. Dad, I wish the enemy knew what I know, that his victory will be shot-lived!"

When we come to the Bible, the first two chapters introduce God as the hero of the universe. God is presented as the invincible, the Almighty God, the creator and sustainer of His creation. However, before long, the enemy introduces himself, and all that God declared to be good is marred by sin, pain and death. As a consequence, there is a flood, slavery of God's people in Egypt; there is the wandering in the wilderness with many losing their lives before the journey's end. By the time of Jeremiah and Habakkuk, there is disobedience and Babylon, and we wonder, what on earth is going on! Is God still in charge?

We have the luxury of going to the last two chapters of the "Book" to see how the cosmic drama will end, and we understand that the God of Genesis, of the beginnings, is the same one who will remain standing at the end. Surely, we know how the drama will end. The last two chapters tell us that God will destroy the enemy and all his works and that God will pay everyone accordingly. We wish the enemy knew that we know how he will end! The enemy will be defeated, and God, the Almighty, will reign forever and ever!

The twenty-first chapter of Revelation takes us to such a time when time shall have surrendered its reign to eternity; when the controversy between God and Satan will come to an end. Revelation's author, John, paints a picture of the climax of God's creative and redemptive powers, when God will put the last signature on what will be taking place. At that time, our prayer, "Your will be done on earth as it is in heaven" (Matthew 6: 10), will be answered in its entirety.

In Revelation 21, once again, John the Revelator describes his vision, which portrayed the reward of the saints and the end of sinners, sin, wickedness, Satan and his angels. He saw a new heaven and a new earth, the end of pollution and all the marks of sin and corruption. He saw the New Jerusalem, the Holy City, descending from heaven with dazzling beauty, which he compares to a bride beautifully prepared to meet her husband. John employed metaphoric language to describe what he saw.

Before John delivered information about the joy and beauty of the new order of things, he looked around to determine if there would be any sea in the New Jerusalem. Before telling us about the joy of the saved and the punishment of the lost, John looked around and declared, "There was no longer any sea!" Why? Some of us we can not imagine a world without seas, oceans, lakes and canals for many reasons:

(a) The seas, oceans and lakes are the homes to many plants and animals on earth. These life forms, with their varied levels of beauty, provide us with a sense of God's creative power. They have been a wonder to the human race throughout ages. Is it then possible to do away with the seas and oceans, and in the process, according to John, do away with God's wonderful creation?

(b) The seas and oceans provide essential transportation for international trade. Most of the world's goods are moved by ships from seaport to seaport, from continent to continent. We have important seaports, lakes, and canals, which provide passages from one point to another.

(c) We have sea foods, and marine animals for aquariums and pets, though global pollution and over-consumption of fish have resulted in seriously decreasing the population of many of the sea and ocean species.

However, we need to remember that John was sea-imprisoned. According to the first chapter of the book of Revelation, John was sentenced by the enemies of the cross and the resurrection, during the persecutions, to be on the island of Patmos, in the Aegean Sea, southwest of Ephesus. At that time, the enemies of the gospel, wanting to silence all the voices of Christ's followers, isolated John, putting him where he could not humanly escape or continue to witness for Christ.

On Patmos John was far from his spiritual brothers and sisters and the Christian church that he loved. Without the warmth of fellowship and the opportunity to testify to the then unbelieving world, on an island without access to transportation, to cross the sea, John longed for a day when this experience would never be repeated. The sea, for John, was a wall of separation, abandonment, loneliness; surrounded by the sea, he was left alone to suffer and die. He became homesick for a city in which "there will be no more sea," no more separation, no more isolation, and no more walls separating God's people. John longed for a city with no walls of partition, no segregation, no more socio-economic classes; a place where God's people would be free indeed.

In that city envisioned by John, all man-made problems would be done away with. Whatever bothers God's children and robs them their peace, like the Aegean Sea, would be taken care of. That sea might be sickness, death, racism, poverty, or loneliness. Writing about his vision of the new city, John says, "There will be no more sea." All the things that threaten to ravage our lives, to overwhelm us, enclose and exclude us would be done away with.

In times of distress, we can read the last chapters of the Book and be assured of the end of our sorrows and pains, and the joy that is ours at the end of the road. Whenever we fail in our efforts to save ourselves from the wiles of the enemy, or from problems we bring upon ourselves by our poor choices, we can be assured that God will not settle for less

The absence of sin and sinners, of Satan and his angels, will also mean the absence of sickness, death, crying and mourning, "for the old order of things" will have passed away (Rev. 21: 4). The New Jerusalem will be a world without coffins, mortuaries, grave yards, and old-age homes, for the residents will be plugged into the source of eternal life; they will be refreshed as eternity rolls.

than saving us from sin, Satan, and from ourselves. Whenever we come to identify with the sufferings of John and of other disciples, we are assured that our suffering and pain, our seas, are transitory, but our joy is forever.

Moreover, in the New Jerusalem, no sea will divide the greatest from the least of the disciples. Between those who conquered nations and those who won a few souls for the kingdom of Christ, there will be no more sea. And there will be no more enemies to put walls between God's children. All God's children will have been washed in the blood; they will have confessed Jesus as Lord and Savior, and be covered by Christ's robe of His righteousness, which He bestowed upon them while they waited on the old earth for Him.

On the other hand, the Bible declares, (Isaiah

57: 20-21) that "the wicked are like the troubled sea, when it cannot rest, whose waters cast up mire and dirt. 'There is no peace,' says my God, 'for the wicked.'" The wicked are as unstable and unpredictable as the sea, which changes and affects those around it with mud, mire, wind, waves and storms, bringing unexpected disasters.

The sea represents, therefore, a state of agitation, restlessness, trouble, lack of safety and security. Like the sea, a sinner affects those near and far by his or her actions. The history of humanity is replete with occasions when a person or group of people threatened the existence of whole tribes or nations. Right after God led His people across the Jordan and directed the destruction of Jericho, Achan sinned against God's commands to seek no loot in Jericho. His sin prevented success for Israel when they battled the people of Ai. Subsequently, all the members of Achan's household, including women and children, were punished with death (Joshua 7). Achan's sin was like "mire and mud," which spoiled the success and peace in Israel, and in his family. Later, whenever sinners and sin multiplied among God's people, He would allow enemies to punish Israel, to take their possessions, killing some, and taking others into captivity as slaves and trophies of the power of the foreign gods. At other times God would allow diseases, drought, confusion and lack of prosperity in all areas of life, until either

His people repented, or only a remnant remained (Deut. 28:15-68; Habakkuk 2). In the process of punishing the sinners in Israel, most of the times the godly suffered alongside with the ungodly.

With the presence of the corrupt, the self-seeking and the unstable on this sin-sick planet earth, ultimate peace is but a dream. On this planet, fear prevails more than love. There is not only fear of what non-believers could do, but even fear of conflicts that may arise between religious communities; for tremendous unrest can arise as a result of religious differences. Whatever sea it is, John still declares "and the sea will be no more." All the works of selfishness and corruption will be banished. All those who have not embraced Christ as their peace when time lingered will be no more, and the divine peace, peace in its fullness, will never be spoiled by the mud from any sea. The war that has been raging throughout human history between what is good and what is evil will be forever ended. Sinners and sin will be no more. The whole creation of God will be clean.

The absence of sin and sinners, of Satan and his angels, will also mean the absence of sickness, death, crying and mourning, "for the old order of things" will have passed away (Rev. 21: 4). The New Jerusalem will be a world without coffins, mortuaries, grave yards, and old-age homes, for the residents will be plugged into the source of eternal life; they will be refreshed as eternity rolls. The promises of the prophet Isaiah (Chapters 60 and 65), which were never realized in the Old Jerusalem, will be fulfilled in the New Jerusalem.

Possessing such wonderful hope of sure fulfill-ment of God's promises, the Christian is blessed with information to share. Is there a true believer anywhere who will not declare, "I wish they [those who have not accepted Jesus as their Savior and Lord] knew what I know is going to happen. I wish the devil understood that I know that he will be no more, and that all the cares and worries of this life will come to an end and there will be peace in the land!" The prophet Isaiah puts these truths in these words:

Chapter 60

18 Violence shall no longer be heard in your land, Neither wasting nor destruction within your borders; But you shall call your walls Salvation, And your gates Praise.

19 "The sun shall no longer be your light by day, Nor for brightness shall the moon give light to you; But the LORD will be to you an everlasting light, And your God your glory.

20 Your sun shall no longer go down, Nor shall your moon withdraw itself; For the LORD will be your everlast-ing light, And the days of your mourning shall be ended.

21 Also your people *shall* all *be* righteous; They shall inherit the land forever, The branch of My planting, The work of My hands, That I may be glorified.

Chapter 65

18 But be glad and rejoice forever in what I create; For behold, I create Jerusalem as a rejoicing, And her people a joy.

19 I will rejoice in Jerusalem, And joy in My people; The voice of weeping shall no longer be heard in her, Nor the voice of crying.

25 The wolf and the lamb shall feed together, The lion shall eat straw like the ox, And dust *shall be* the serpent's food. They shall not hurt nor destroy in all My holy mountain," Says the LORD.

We wait for the coming King with hope, faith and love, which enable us to live above our vicissitudes while still here on planet earth. As pilgrims, one artist, Eliza Edmunds Hewitt, admonishes us to sing a song that "will cheer us by the way," for in a little while we will be going home. She is one of those who labored for the Lord and did not give up during her sickness.[1] She looked forward to a city where sickness and death will be no more. There will be no more sea in the New Jerusalem. Here is her song:

"In a Little While We're Going Home"

Let us sing a song that will cheer us by the way,
In a little while we're going home;
For the night will end in the everlasting day,
In a little while we're going home.

<u>Chorus</u>
In a little while, In a little while,
We shall cross the billow's foam;
We shall meet at last, When the stormy winds are past,
In a little while we're going home.

We will do the work that our hands may find to do,
In a little while we're going home;
And the grace of God will our daily strength renew,
In a little while we're going home.

We will smooth the path for some weary, way-worn feet,
In a little while we're going home;
And may loving hearts spread around an influence sweet!
In a little while we're going home.

There's a rest beyond, there's relief from every care,
In a little while we're going home;
And no tears shall fall in that city bright and fair,
In a little while we're going home.

Notes

Chapter One
Challenges are Common Denominators

1. Marakakgoro, Mmereki. (n.d.). Eet-Sum-More. A music cassette recorded at Joy Records. The song that is cited, "When the going is tough," is the first on the second side of the tape, composed by Mmereki Marakakgoro.

Chapter Two
His Grace is Sufficient

1. Osbeck, K.W. (1982). 101 Hymn Stories: the Inspiring True Stories Behind 101 Favorite Hymns. Kregel Publications, MI., (p.147).

Chapter Three
The Power of His Cross

1. White, E. G. (1940). The Desire of Ages. Pacific Press Publishing Association, Mountain View, California.

2. Weigle, Charles Frederick lived between 1871 and 1966. It is said he composed the song, "No One Ever Cared for Me Like Jesus," during one of his darkest periods of his life. The story behind this song was goggled in 2009 by the author of this book and this is the website: http://www.my.homewithgod.com/mkcathy2/inspirational3/weigle.html

Chapter Four
The Power of His Resurrection

1. White, E. G. (1940). The Desire of Ages. Pacific Press Publishing Association, Mountain View, California.

2. Calvary Singers. (1998). I'm On the Train. Music cassette, recorded at Mafikeng, South Africa. "Learn to Trust in Him" is sung by this music group, Calvary Singers, and the song was composed by Boitumelo Rakwena in 1995.

Chapter Five
The Just Shall Live by Faith

1. Hills, D. B. (1981). Light for My Life.
   Review and Herald Publishing Association,
   Washington, D. C.

Chapter Six
He Tested Abraham's Faith

1. Harris, R. L., Archer, Jr., G. L. & Waltke, B.
   K. (1980). Theological Wordbook of the Old
   Testament, Volume 2. Moody Press, Chicago.

2. Nichol, F. D., Cottrell, R. F. & Neuffer, J. (1978).
   The Seventh-day Adventist Bible Commentary,
   Volume 1. Review and Herald Publishing
   Association, Washington, D. C.

3. Harris, R. L., Archer, Jr., G. L. & Waltke, B.
   K. (1980). Theological Wordbook of the Old
   Testament, Volume 2. Moody Press, Chicago.

4. Osbeck, K.W. (1982). 101 Hymn Stories:
   the Inspiring True Stories Behind 101 Favorite
   Hymns. Kregel Publications, MI., (pp. 25-26).

Chapter Seven
Do You Also Want to Go Away

1. Hooper, Wayne and White, Edward E. (1988). Companion to the Seventh-day Adventist Hymnal. Review and Herald Publishing Association, Hagerstown, MD (p. 574).

Chapter Eight
Jehoshaphat and His Enemies

1. Daniel Speaks Ministries. (2007). Ha ke Timeletse .... Music CD, recorded at Mud Hut Studios, Gaborone, Botswana. "God is our Shelter" is sung by this music group, Daniel Speaks, and the group credits Segaetsho as the composer of this song.
Go

Chapter Nine
Challenges are Like a Quarry

1. Pargament, K.I. (1997). The psychology of religion and coping: Theory, research, and practice. New York: Guiford.

2. Rakwena, Boitumelo. (2006). Religious coping among people of individuals with HIV/AIDS. (Master's theses, Loma Linda University, 2006).

3. Swindoll, C. R. (1982). Strengthening your Grip: Essentials in an Aimless World. Word Books Publisher, Texas, (p. 207).

4. Osbeck, K.W. (1982). 101 Hymn Stories: The Inspiring True Stories Behind 101 Favorite Hymns. Kregel Publications, MI., (pp. 126-128).

Chapter Ten
No More Sea

1. Hooper, Wayne and White, Edward E. (1988). Companion to the Seventh-day Adventist Hymnal. Review and Herald Publishing Association, Hagerstown, MD (pp. 575, 639).